GOTCHA

Edited by John Essery,

with a Foreword by Kelvin MacKenzie

A SIGNET BOOK

Foreword by Kelvin MacKenzie

The front page of the *Sun* is one of the world's great shop windows. Every morning almost 10 million people study it and decide whether to buy. No other English-language paper on Earth has pulling power like that. So what makes a memorable *Sun* front page? Is there a magic formula? In a way there is. For on the wall of the *Sun*'s editorial floor is a sign which proclaims:

News is anything which makes the reader say 'Gee whiz'.

That is our aim. Day by day, week after week.

For twenty-four years the *Sun* has made people sit up and take notice. They never know what emotion each morning's paper will bring: anger, laughter, tears, outrage.

It may be a headline that captures the mood of the nation. It may be a picture that tugs at the heartstrings. It may be an outrageous pun or a zany stunt. The only thing that's certain is that with the *Sun* nothing is certain. Surprise is the key.

This book is an insight into the creativity of our headline writers and a tribute to the boldness of men and women who tell it like it is. On the *Sun* we don't pull punches. That's why so many people swear by us – and a few others swear at us.

But no one ignores us.

BATTLE FOR THE ISLANDS

STICK IT UP YOUR JUNTA

1am: Maggie No to deal—then Argentina invokes war treaty

★ **BRITISH** envoy Richard Hardy shares a smile with his 24-year-old Argentine bride Astrid Posse after their wedding in Buenos Aires.

The couple planned to marry next month, but rushed the ceremony through yesterday because of the Falklands crisis which divides their countries.

LOVE CONQUERS ALL FOR ENVOY

PREMIER Margaret Thatcher called a Falklands war cabinet last night — and quickly gave a frosty answer to Argentina's latest peace moves.

As talking finished in the early hours, the British

By WALTER TERRY and CHRISTOPHER POTTER

response was clearly: Stick it up your junta !

A statement from Downing Street said that the Fascist rulers' proposals "did not meet the requirements strongly expressed by Parliament."

Argentina immediately hit back by calling on every South American country to come to their defence.

The Junta announced it is to ask for an urgent meeting of the Organisation of American States to invoke the Treaty of Rio — a Nato-style defence pact.

This could mean that the 21 member countries — including the United States —are obliged to give military support.

Tory Party chairman Cecil Parkinson was summoned to the crisis meeting.

He warned Mrs Thatcher that it would almost certainly mean the end of her Premiership if she backed down.

JOINED

The Premier summoned her big guns as U.S. troubleshooter Alexander Haig flew from Buenos Aires to Washington, after sending details of Argentina's peace proposals to London.

She was joined by Home Secretary William

Peace envoy Haig yesterday . . . flying back to Washington

Continued on Page Two

THE Sun

Tuesday, May 4, 1982   14p   TODAY'S TV: PAGE 12

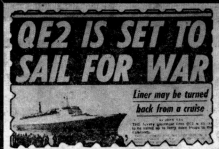

QE2 IS SET TO SAIL FOR WAR

Liner may be turned back from a cruise

By JOHN KAY

THE luxury passenger liner QE2 is still to be called up to ferry more troops to the Falklands...

We told you first

NINE days ago The Sun said that the QE2 was to be called up. Everybody denied it. Yesterday the Ministry of Defence confirmed it. If you really want to know what's going on in the war buy The Sun. We try harder. See Page 2

GOTCHA

Our lads sink gunboat and hole cruiser

From TONY SNOW aboard HMS Invincible

THE NAVY had the Argies on their knees last night after a devastating double punch.

WALLOP: They torpedoed the 14,000-ton Argentina cruiser General Belgrano and left it a useless wreck.

WALLOP: Task Force helicopters sank one Argentine patrol boat and severely damaged another.

The Belgrano, which survived the Pearl Harbour attack when it belonged to the U.S. Navy, had been asking for trouble all day.

The cruiser, second largest in the Argy fleet, had been skirting the 200-mile war zone that Britain has set up around the Falkland Islands.

MAJOR

With its 15 six-inch guns our Navy high command were certain that it would have played a major part in any battle to retain the Falklands.

But the Belgrano and

its 1,000 crew needn't worry about the war for some time now.

For the nuclear submarine Conqueror, captained by Commander Richard Wraith, let fly with two torpedoes.

The ship was not sunk and it is not clear how many casualties there were.

HMS Conqueror was built at Cammell Laird's shipyard in Birkenhead for £30million. She was launched in 1969 and *Continued on Page Two*

SUNK — AN Argie patrol boat like this one was sunk by missiles from Royal Navy helicopters after first opening fire on our lads

CRIPPLED — THE Argie cruiser General Belgrano . . . put out of action by Tigerfish torpedoes from our super nuclear sub Conqueror

UNION BOYCOTTS WAR

A UNION chief is telling seamen on two ships taken over by the Government: "Don't go to war—the union can't protect you."

The astonishing advice comes from George Cartwright, the Communist leader of the National Union of Seamen at Felixstowe Port in Suffolk.

The Government has just requisitioned the Townsend Thoresen roll-on, roll-off vessels Baltic Ferry and Nordic Ferry.

'Folly'

The ferries will carry troops and battle equipment in support of the QE2.

Mr Cartwright told the 150 seamen: "Our advice is that it would be folly to go off on a dangerous adventure.

"I'm old enough to remember that one in three merchant seamen were killed in the last war.

"It is not a case of being unpatriotic. We are not at war and our advice is based on union practicalities.

"W[h]at we are saying is that if seamen put themselves under military command, they will no longer have our protection."

He believes the majority of crew members will decide not to sail to the South Atlantic.

"So far I have heard from three seamen who want to go, the rest are non-commital or against joining the task force," Mr Cartwright said.

Question

"There is no question of politics being behind the recommendation. We were asked for our view and gave our best advice."

BATTLE FOR THE ISLANDS

£50,000 BINGO! Today's lucky numbers are on Page 20

THE Sun

Saturday, May 29, 1982   14p   **THE PAPER THAT SUPPORTS OUR BOYS**

VICTORY

Paras rout Argies to seize Darwin and Goose Green

By BRIAN WOOSEY

BRITAIN'S Para heroes captured Darwin and Goose Green last night in the bitter battle for the Falklands.

Bayonets fixed, they wrested the key enemy strongholds from the Argies following fierce hand-to-hand fighting.

Seven hundred men of the 2nd Battalion Parachute Regiment stormed the twin towns at dusk, taking many prisoners.

And the victories put them on course to recapture the islands' capital Port Stanley.

RESISTANCE

The daring exploits of the British troops mean we have now regained the vital airstrip at Goose Green.

The 1,000 Argies defending the strategic centres—just two miles apart at the head of the Choiseul Sound—put up a fierce resistance.

But the battle was over in less than 36 hours—with heavy casualties inflicted on the enemy. British casualties were light, a Defence spokesman said last night.

Darwin and Goose Green are the first settlements to fall since our 5,000 troops landed on the Falklands last Friday.

Earlier, the land battles took their toll of British troops.

KILLED

Four Marines and a Royal Engineer were killed and up to 20 badly wounded after Argy jets attacked on Thursday.

The 2nd Battalion are led by plain-speaking tough-guy Lieutenant Colonel Herbert Jones—known simply as "H" to his colleagues.

Action man "H" has served in Aden, Borneo and Northern Ireland.

MARCHING OFF TO WAR . . . the heroes of the 2nd Battalion Parachute Regiment leave their HQ

PARAS STORM TO GLORY   Pages 2 and 3

THE Sun

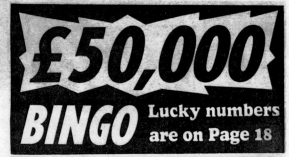

£50,000 BINGO
Lucky numbers are on Page 18

FREDDIE STARR ATE MY HAMSTER

Sickened . . . animal-loving Lea yesterday   Picture: PETER RALPH

Freddie . . . "It's lies"

Comic put a live pet in sandwich, says beauty

EXCLUSIVE by DICK SAXTY

ZANY comic Freddie Starr put a live hamster in a sandwich and ATE it, model girl Lea La Salle claimed yesterday.

She said "I was sickened and horrified. He killed my pet.

"It's something I'll never forget. He put my hamster between two slices of bread and started eating it.

"He thought it was hilarious,"said Lea. "He just fell about laughing."

Lea, 23, said the incident—which Starr hotly denies—happened while the comic was staying with her and boyfriend Vincent McCaffrey in Birchwood, Cheshire. Freddie was performing at a Manchester nightclub.

Lea, a former Miss UK runner-up, said: "He used to get back in the early hours and demand something to eat.

"On about the fifth night, I told him to get something himself.

BITE

"He came back from the kitchen with a sandwich, and at first I didn't pay any attention to what was in it. I saw him take a bite.

"Then I saw part of my hamster Supersonic sticking out from between the bread."

Supersonic was kept in an open-top glass cage near the kitchen, said Lea.

"I screamed when I

Continued on Page Seven

SELLERS GIRL IS

Vicky . . . police hunt

CHARGED IN DRUG CASE

Page 5

JEWEL IN MY CROWN

Vicar praises rape daughter

By MURIEL BURDEN

THE vicar whose daughter was raped by the "spidermen" gang praised the 21-year-old girl's courage last night.

With tears in his eyes he said: "She is the jewel in my crown."

The vicar, whose skull was fractured in the attack, was speaking from his hospital bed as police were early today quizzing FIVE men and a WOMAN about the crime.

He said: "I am deeply impressed with the way my daughter and her boyfriend have responded to the situation."

Justice

The girl's boyfriend was also beaten unconscious during the attack in a West London vicarage.

Of the men, the vicar said: "I want to see justice done. I think this country is soft on justice.

"But not once have I felt hatred or felt vengeful I feel sad for them. They were a trio of derelicts.

"And if I am a Christian minister, preaching a gospel of reconciliation and hope for the outcasts of this world, I would have no gospel if I did not have that in my heart.

"Clergymen are supposed to be plaster saints. But I can say that in all honesty, not because I am a clergyman, but as a man who has been bashed up."

Thousands of messages and cards have been sent to the vicarage in six days since the attack.

The vicar added: "I will not be able to write personally to everyone. But I hope they will take this as my deep appreciation of their kind words and thoughts."

Two of the men being ques-

Continued on Page Two

THE Sun

Saturday, May 10, 1986   **18p**   **TODAY'S TV IS ON PAGE 14**

GOSH! Geisha girl Princess Diana slips into a kimono yesterday during her visit to Japan with Prince Charles . . . and the Jap wrap makes her look just like a character from the Oriental opera Madam Butterfly!

Full story—Page Five

SWEET FA FOR 25,000 FANS

Chaos over Cup tickets

By DICK SAXTY and JOHN KAY

AN ANGRY army of 25,000 soccer fans is threatening to cause havoc at today's Merseyside Cup Final at Wembley.

The red-and-blue mob was last night converging on the stadium without a genuine ticket between them.

Many were clutching forgeries which they hope will fool stewards on the turnstiles.

Others had phoney tickets they bought in innocence. But stadium chiefs insisted last night: "We have the men and the equipment to detect the forgeries and we are confident we will spot them all."

Worried police fear there could be big trouble when the desperate supporters are turned away to rampage around outside the stadium.

Massive reinforcements will be on duty and extra stewards have been drafted in. A mass exodus of 75,000

Continued on Page Two

£50,000 BINGO! Winner and today's lucky numbers—Page 10

THE Sun

Monday, May 12, 1986   18p   TODAY'S TV IS ON PAGE 14

QUEEN NICKS CASTLE DRUNK

She saw ex-guardsman wee by a tree

★ IT'S the tender kiss that says "welcome home" to sailing superstar Simon Le Bon from his lovely wife Yasmin. The couple spent minutes locked in an emotional embrace yesterday after the Duran Duran singer finished third in the Whitbread round-the-world race with his yacht Drum.

★ Yasmin, 21, waited hours at the Portsmouth quayside for her hero's return. And she had to kick her heels for another 40 minutes while customs officers searched Drum for drugs. But they found nothing.

Picture: HARRY PAGE

HELLO SAILOR

SUN EXCLUSIVE

By JOHN ASKILL

A DRUNKEN former royal guardsman was behind bars last night . . . after being shopped by the Queen.

She was **NOT** amused when she spotted Tommy O'Boyle relieving himself by a tree at the roadside as she drove home to Windsor Castle after taking tea with the Queen Mum.

The Queen was so shocked by the royal wee that she reported the incident to a guard at the castle gate, and police immediately swooped to arrest 46-year-old O'Boyle.

Yesterday the ex-Irish Guardsman, who once paraded in royal ceremonies at Windsor and Buckingham Palace, was spending his **THIRD** night behind bars.

O'Boyle travelled to Windsor from his home in Newport, Gwent, on Friday to have a few

Continued on Page Seven

Tommy O'Boyle ... locked up

£50,000 BINGO! Winners and numbers—Page 7

THE Sun

£50,000

BINGO! Today's lucky numbers-Page 24

Thursday, July 17, 1986   18p   **TODAY'S TV IS ON PAGE 14**

DI AND FERGIE POSE AS GIRL COPS

Arresting pair . . . The Sun's impression of how Princess Diana and Sarah Ferguson might look in uniform

Giggling Royal pals
in nightclub prank

By HARRY ARNOLD

ROYAL bride Sarah Ferguson and her pal Princess Diana posed as policewomen in an amazing hen-party stunt at a nightclub, it was revealed last night.

The daring duo—both wearing wigs and dressed in hired uniforms—bluffed their way in, walked boldly up to the bar and ordered Cokes.

Then the giggling Royal pranksters moved to a table in a dark corner of the upper-crust London club Annabel's.

DISGUISES

Di and Fergie were with a third girl—believed to be TV funnygirl Pamela Stephenson—who flashed a "warrant card" to get them past doormen.

Their disguises were so perfect that people in the club were convinced at first they were genuine WPCs.

Diana was wearing glasses and a long black wig over her blonde tresses. Sarah hid her distinctive flame-coloured hair beneath a short brown hairpiece.

But after 20 minutes, rumours started going round the nightspot's staff about the real identities of the cute cops.

As people began to stare, the jokers realised the game was up—and made for the door.

The arrival of the three "policewomen" at Annabel's was seen by *Continued on Page Two*

FERGIE GETS THE ABBEY HABIT Centre Pages

ENOCH RAPS QUEEN

By TREVOR KAVANAGH

ENOCH POWELL warned the Queen yesterday to keep out of the looming storm over South African sanctions.

Mr Powell, an authority on the British Constitution, claimed Her Majesty has no right to intervene in the political row at next month's Commonwealth summit.

The Ulster MP attacked as a "scoundrel" the senior Minister he says has leaked details of the Queen's view on sanctions.

The rift between Downing Street and the Palace has developed rapidly as the Queen—head of the Commonwealth—comes under pressure from black African leaders to intervene. Mr Powell

dismissed the Commonwealth as "humbug" and said no one in Britain would complain if it disbanded.

"The Sovereign understands perfectly well that, as a constitutional monarch, she acts in this country on the advice of her Ministers," said Mr Powell, the *Continued on Page Two*

Enoch . . . warning

ROYAL Sun

Thursday, July 24, 1986 ★ ★ ★ ★

QUEEN DOES A RUNNER

Panic . . . the Queen breaks into a sprint to catch Prince Willie

By **JOHN KAY** and **KEVIN O'SULLIVAN**

THE Queen was forced to do a runner yesterday to stop playful Prince William hurting himself—as he tried to join Andy and Fergie on their honeymoon!

The 60-year-old monarch did not hesitate to break into a sprint to grab Willie as he trotted after the newlyweds' coach, dangerously close to its massive rear wheels.

It was the first time in recent memory that anyone had seen her run.

The moment of panic came after Andy and Fergie boarded the 1902 State Landau to set off from Buckingham Palace on the first leg of their honeymoon journey.

Four-year-old Willie, who had wedding guests in hysterics all day with his antics, climbed in with them.

His mum Princess Di told him to get down. Willie did as he was told, but then slipped Di's grasp to chase the coach.

The Queen, spotting the danger instantly, dashed after him for several yards before holding him back.

One amazed Palace official said: "It was an incredible sight.

CONFETTI

"Many of us have worked here for years and we have never seen the Queen run before."

Fergie, dressed in a white silk dress printed with violet flowers, shed a tear of joy as she was showered with confetti by Di and other royals.

And she blew kisses to the crowd as she and Andy rode to the Royal Hospital in Chelsea.

A helicopter took them from there to Heathrow Airport. And a Queen's Flight jet whisked them on to the Azores in mid-Atlantic.

But before they took off, two videos of the wedding ceremony were rushed to them by a motorbike despatch rider.

IT'S A TEDDY FROM EDDIE

ANDY and Fergie leave for their honeymoon-...with a Teddy from Eddie.

Clown Prince Edward strapped the giant bear—smartly-dressed in a blue bow-tie ribbon—into the newlyweds' coach before they pulled away from Buckingham Palace.

The prankster Prince, Andy's "best man" at the wedding, shelled out £500 for his parting trick. A member of the Palace staff said last night: "The Prince told the couple they might need something to hug on their honeymoon. Everyone thought it was a great laugh."

Edward also tied a placard to the back of the Landau bearing the ET film catchprase: Phone Home!

Picture: PETER SIMPSON

Printed by London Post (Printers) Ltd., 1 Virginia Street, London E1. © News Group Newspapers Ltd. Registered as a newspaper at the Post Office No. 5,197. Chan is 19p, Spain 130pts, Can is 125pts, Malta 16 cents.

THE Sun

Wednesday, January 7, 1987   18p   TODAY'S TV IS ON PAGE 10

ELTON'S AGONY AFTER OP

STRICKEN rock star Elton John was in agony last night after an operation to find out whether he has cancer of the throat.

Elton, 39, has been forced to use pen and paper to communicate with visitors at the exclusive St Vincent's private hospital in Sydney.

He will not be able to sing again for several months.

Friends said he was resting comfortably after the 75-minute exploratory operation and scribbling cheerful notes to hospital staff.

Elton's 5 days of fear —See Pages Four and Five

Elton . . . cancer worry

I QUIT

Marines' badge of courage

Weeping Edward wants to pack in too-tough Marines

Action man . . . Edward swings into training before his decision to quit

By JOHN KAY

PRINCE Edward sensationally quit the Royal Marines yesterday—because he found the commando training too tough.

Edward, 22, cried for three hours after making up his mind last Friday to leave the crack fighting force.

The Prince, the Queen's youngest son, drafted his letter of resignation after just four months full-time training towards winning the commandos' coveted Green Beret.

Prince Philip, the Marines' honorary Captain General, had a furious row with Edward over his decision.

He was said to have shouted at Edward and told him to pull himself together to spare the Royal Family embarrassment.

The Queen was also reported

Sun world exclusive

to be deeply upset over Edward's decision.

Yesterday the Marines' commanding officer, Commandant General Sir Michael Wilkins, spent two hours at Buckingham Palace begging Edward to change his mind.

Edward thrust a letter of resignation at Sir Michael—but he refused to accept it and asked Edward to think again.

He told him it was the Prince's duty to stay on with the Marines and complete his 12-month officers' training course. Edward

was due to report back to the commandos' training base at Lympstone, Devon, on Monday after the Christmas break.

But Buckingham Palace officials told officers that the Prince was suffering from a bout of flu.

After his meeting with Sir Michael, Edward agreed to travel to Lympstone today for talks with senior officers.

RESIGNED

He will start the "counselling process" which every marine who wants to quit the commandos has to undergo. Top brass will make a final bid to persuade the Prince to change his mind.

But both Sir Michael and Prince Philip were said to be resigned to Edward quitting.

The Prince has decided to pull out because he finds the training programme too tough and demanding.

He has also become disillu-

Continued on Page Two

THE HELL OF BEING A MARINE — See Page 9

THE Sun

Wednesday, March 22, 1989   **20p**   Yesterday's sale: 4,266,826   Thought: That's tough, Derrick

A LOAD OF BOLLARDS

Driver jailed over parking as Royals went to wedding

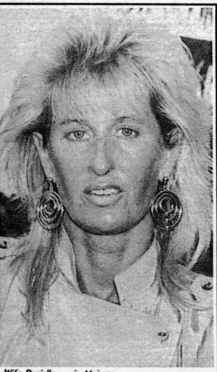

Wife Danielle ... in Majorca   **Picture by HARRY PAGE**

MOTORIST Derrick Gibbs was locked in a top security jail last night ... because he parked his van near a wedding attended by Royals.

Stubborn Derrick, 44, refused police requests to move it from outside his house when Diana and Fergie arrived for the high society bash nearby.

And yesterday magistrates sentenced the builder to five days in **PRISON**, after he refused to pay a £15 fine for ignoring temporary no-parking bollards.

Shocked pals watched in horror as Derrick, who claims to be a fan of the Royals, was led away in handcuffs.

HOUSE

And last night he was in Leicester jail — a maximum security prison for dangerous criminals.

Derrick's friend Olivia Pope raged: "It's absolutely ridiculous! You can't send a man to

By JOHN ASKILL

jail for parking outside his own home.

"He's parked in the same spot for three years."

The trouble began just before the wedding of Royal pal Susie Murray-Philipson and merchant banker Alexander Dolby in September last year.

Police slapped "no parking" bollards outside Derrick's house 60 yards from the church in Uppingham, Leics. But the

Continued on Page Two

Derrick ... wouldn't pay

THE Sun

Friday, October 27, 1989   **22p**   Audited daily sale for September: 4,113,114   Thought: Pity about Sir Alan

HATED by homeowners
HATED by big business
HATED by the little guy
(At last HE'S done something right)

GOODBYE AND GOOD RIDDANCE

By SIMON WALTERS

CHANCELLOR Nigel Lawson — the man hated by all Britain — finally did the right thing last night and quit.

His sensational resignation plunged Premier Margaret Thatcher into her greatest crisis.

But his going will mean rejoicing for **HOME-BUYERS** crippled by soaring mortgage repayments.

It will also bring joy to **BIG BUSINESS** and **LITTLE MAN** alike — struggling under the burden of sky-high interest rates.

Mr Lawson decided it was time to go because of the seething feud over Mrs Thatcher's economic guru Sir Alan Walters.

Throughout a day of political bombshells, the Prime Minister tried three times to persuade Mr Lawson to stay.

But soon after she defended both men in the Commons, Mr Lawson announced to the world that he had had enough.

He told Mrs Thatcher he could no longer carry on while Sir Alan remained as her personal economic adviser.

SLUMP

Then Sir Alan, hearing the news on a lecture tour in Florida, phoned to say he was "deeply shocked" — and **QUIT** himself.

The crisis rocked the City. The pound fell six pfennigs against the German mark to DM 2.90. Shares are expected to slump when trading opens today.

Foreign Secretary John Major was appointed new Chancellor as Mrs Thatcher

Continued on Page Two

Lawson . . . resignation plunges Tories into crisis

AIRMAN AND BABY SHOT DEAD BY IRA - Page 11

THE Sun

Friday, November 10, 1989 **22p** Estimated daily sale for October: 4,036,550 Thought: Red letter day'

WAR PLANE HITS FLATS

DOZENS of people were feared dead last night after a military jet crashed into a block of flats and started a massive blaze.

The pilot parachuted from the doomed plane as it dived towards an apartment complex in Atlanta, Georgia.

An eye-witness said: "You can see the flames lighting up the sky. We are sure there will be many dead and injured."

—See Page Two

IT'S WALL OVER

Berlin carnival as Iron Curtain falls

By TREVOR KAVANAGH and JOHN HELLINGS

THE hated Berlin Wall was thrown wide open last night — and hundreds of jubilant East Germans surged across to be greeted by champagne and fireworks in the West.

East Berliners crying with joy burst through checkpoints to celebrate their freedom with new-found friends on the other side.

The Wall — symbol of tyranny and a barrier between East and West for 28 years — was overwhelmed by crowds in carnival spirit.

It now seems certain to be pulled down. West Berliners chanted, "The Wall is gone, The Wall is gone" after Communist leaders announced they were removing the last restrictions on their citizens leaving East Germany.

Many East Berliners walked through to the West then **RETURNED** — just to prove their new freedom was real.

One woman came back and said: "Going to West Berlin was as good as going to Australia for me."

Crowds, whooping and cheering like soccer fans, converged on the Bornholmer Strasse crossing point.

Drivers in a half-mile queue of cars tooted their horns incessantly.

GUARDS

Pedestrians yelled: "We're off to the Kudamm" — West Berlin's main boulevard.

The eight crossing points were not supposed to be officially opened until today — but guards could do little

West Berliners stormed Checkpoint Charlie to prove the freedom was two-way and shouted "We want in" at Continued on Page Seven

The brave who made it and those who didn't -Pages 6 & 7

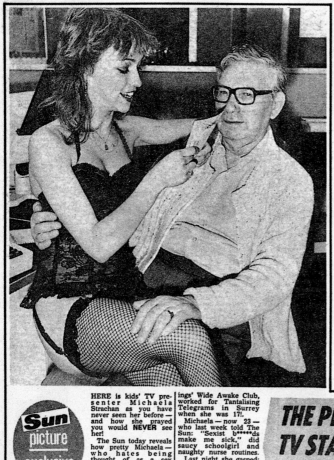

HERE is kids' TV presenter Michaela Strachan as you have never seen her before — and how she prayed you would **NEVER** see her!

The Sun today reveals how pretty Michaela — who hates being thought of as a sex object — once worked as a £15-a-night **STRIPPOGRAM** girl.

The children's favourite in Saturday morn- ings' Wide Awake Club, worked for Tantalising Telegrams in Surrey when she was 17!.

Michaela — now 23 — who last week told The Sun: "Sexist b*****ds make me sick," did saucy schoolgirl and naughty nurse routines.

Last night she gasped: "Oh God — I prayed these photos would never get out."

Michaela Strip-an — Centre Pages

THE PHOTO KIDS' TV STAR PRAYED YOU'D NEVER SEE

£54,000 LOTTO:—See Page 11 ● £31,000 BINGO:—See Page 20

THE Sun

Thursday, November 23, 1989   **22p**   Audited daily sale for October: 4,039,509   Thought: Is it George Bushy?

Minister calls for Maggie loyalty tests

By TREVOR KAVANAGH and SIMON WALTERS

TORY MPs were urged last night to take a "loyalty test" to prove they back Margaret Thatcher's party leadership.

Energy minister Peter Morrison spearheaded the call, praising the Prime Minister's "enormous achievements."

He said: "I hope, over the next few days, every other member of the Government will be making similar declarations."

The move came as dissident MP Sir Anthony Meyer prepared to challenge Mrs Thatcher next month as Tory leader.

Mr Morrison said in a letter to his constituency bosses at Chester: "I will be voting for Mrs

SHE'S 3-1 ON

MRS Thatcher is a 3-1 ON hot favourite with bookies William Hill to lead the Tories at the next General Election. They offer 2-1 against her being replaced by then.

Thatcher and supporting her in every way."

He said constituency chiefs should ask their MPs how they would vote in a leadership poll.

Mr Morrison added: "Unless they get a straight answer that it will be only for Mrs Thatcher, then they should make their MPs understand the implications."

Mrs Thatcher also slapped down rebels set on dumping her, with the message: Put up, or shut up. She signalled she

Continued on Page Two

GOOSE STEP GOES

The Nazi-style goose step used by East German troops at parades has been banned by new, reforming defence chief Theodor Hoffmann.

GLASNUTS

Nuts go west . . . Mikhail Gorbachev watches intently as a red squirrel eats a free treat from his hand in Moscow

WORLD EXCLUSIVE PICTURE

Gorbachev treat for Red squirrel

A HUNGRY squirrel shows no fear as Mikhail Gorbachev offers the hand of friendship . . . and a free meal of nuts.

A camera captured this magic moment as

By SHAN LANCASTER

the Russian leader relaxed in the grounds of his country dacha near Moscow.

Warm-hearted Gorby spotted the squirrel — a red one of course — as it scampered nearby. And

within seconds, he had it eating out of his hand.

Gorby watched in wonderment as his new pal tucked into its nutty treat. Clearly, the new climate of glasnost sweeping aside the Iron Curtain even extends to our furry friends.

Magic Moment — Page Nine

THE Sun

Wednesday, February 7, 1990 **22p**   Yesterday's estimated sale: 4,016,829   Thought: Nice work...

BILLY IDOL IN OP TO SAVE LEG

From ALLAN HALL in New York

SURGEONS were last night battling to save rock wildman Billy Idol's leg after it was shattered in a horrific motorbike smash.

Billy, 34, was in a Los Angeles operating theatre for three hours and was listed as "critical."

His right leg was broken in several places when his powerful Harley Davidson bike hit a car in Hollywood.

Witnesses claimed the former star of Generation X punk band **JUMPED** a red traffic light and was not wearing a crash helmet.

Miraculously he es-

Continued on Page Three

Billy ... fight to save leg

ONE LAWSON FOR THE RICH

Blackadder weds his TV beauty in secret

By NICK PARKER

BLACKADDER star Rowan Atkinson has secretly married his former TV make-up girl, it was revealed yesterday.

Rowan, 34, wed long-time girlfriend Sunetra Sastry, 24, in a quickie civil ceremony in New York at the weekend.

The rubber-faced comic's only guest was his TV co-star Stephen Fry, who was best man.

Afterwards, the trio celebrated with caviar and champagne at the £100-a-head Russian Tea Rooms restaurant in Manhattan.

Award

Rowan met Asian beauty Sunetra — who worked on make-up for Blackadder — three years ago. He popped the question in Switzerland last year.

Early yesterday the couple flew back to Britain in time for Rowan to collect an award as BBC TV Personality of the Year.

He sat red-faced among 800 guests as they were told the happy news.

Last night he quipped: "I didn't want a massive wedding — so I kept guests to just the one close friend.

"It was a very cosy affair and I'm absolutely delighted."

Newly-weds ... Rowan with Sunetra   Picture by ROGER CRUMP

Fury as he grabs another £40,000

By DAVID KEMP

FORMER Chancellor Nigel Lawson was slammed yesterday for accepting ANOTHER lucrative part-time job.

A storm of protest greeted news that he will be paid £40,000 a year for working just two or three days a month with Irish aircraft leasing firm GPA.

Last week, Mr Lawson, 57, was named as a director of Barclays Bank, where he will earn £175,000 a year for a two-day week.

Criticism was led by Queen's Chaplain Canon John Grimwade.

In a rare outburst, he **DENOUNCED** Mr Lawson for trying to impose one law on the poor when he was Chancellor — only to adopt another himself.

POACHER

Canon Grimwade also accused moneybags Mr Lawson of encouraging inflation and setting a rotten example.

Mr Lawson's latest job takes his annual income close to £250,000 — including the £26,701 he earns as back-bench Tory MP for Blaby.

He quit as Chancellor last year after a row with Premier Margaret Thatcher over her adviser Sir Alan Walters, and stands to make £500,000 from his memoirs.

In a BBC radio interview, Canon Grimwade said: "This is inciting other people to want big increases which fuels inflation even further.

"Sometimes it's the poacher who turns gamekeeper — it looks a bit the other way around at the moment."

Chris Pond, director of the Low Pay Unit, branded Mr Lawson's new job "scandalous."

He said: "This is the man who by his high-interest rate policy pushed many part-time workers into debt." And Labour Treasury spokesman Chris Smith demanded: "What with Barclays, his memoirs and yet another directorship, how will he have time to look after his constituents?"

Mr Lawson refused to comment.

£312,000 No, not Nigel's pay .. it's Sun Lotto—Page 4

THE Sun

Tuesday, February 20, 1990 **22p**   Yesterday's estimated sale: 4,035,262   Thought: Browne and out

Gaunt . . . Freddie leaves the party

A RIGHT B'STARD

Cover-up Tory MP faces sack over Arab cash

Browne . . "excuses strained credulity"

CRASH KILLS 4

A MUM and two children died when a stolen Sierra rammed their car yesterday.

Janice Townsend, 35, son Lucas, 8, and Oliver Rouse, three, lived in Rugby.

Sierra driver George Johnston, 41, of Coventry, also died. Another mum and three more kiddies were hurt in the crash at Ryton, Warwicks.

By TREVOR KAVANAGH
Political Editor

TORY MP John Browne was branded a right B'Stard last night — just like the character in the TV series.

He was found guilty by fellow MPs of cashing in on his Parliamentary role.

Mr Browne, like actor Rik Mayall's Alan B'Stard in TV's The New Statesman, used his status to boost private deals.

And just like scoundrel B'Stard, some of his excuses "strained credulity," a powerful Commons committee ruled.

After a "trial" lasting nine months, ex-Army captain Browne was found guilty of three counts of breaking Commons anti-corruption rules. The committee's report demanded urgent action against him by the Commons. Mrs Thatcher must now decide

whether to suspend him or force a by-election in his Winchester constituency by kicking him out.

The committee ruled that Mr Browne, 51, failed to reveal:

● A £2,400-A-YEAR fee from Lebanese middlemen helping a British firm win an order for a Middle East petrol plant.

BITTER

He was at the time lobbying Ministers on the firm's behalf.

● A PAYMENT to him of 88,000 dollars — about £52,000 — by Saudi Arabia for a report on freezing Iranian assets after the U.S. Embassy siege in Teheran.

He questioned Mrs Thatcher on the Iranian issue.

● LIKELY financial gains when he spoke in a Commons debate on cable TV. The inquiry probed hundreds of documents. Browne claims they were maliciously provided through his ex-wife, Elizabeth.

Some of the papers featured in their bitter divorce where Elizabeth accused him of adultery and ended up being ordered to pay **HIM** a £175,000 settlement.

When she could not complete it, he tried to have her jailed, and this month, the once-wealthy heiress was declared bankrupt. French-born Elizabeth said in London last night: "At last I am seeing justice done. This is partly thanks to us having a free Press.

"I suffered greatly from non-disclosures by John Browne. I lost my home. The judge be-

Continued on Page Two

By PIERS MORGAN

SINGER Freddie Mercury looks gaunt and pale as he leaves a star-studded party held to honour him and his Queen pals.

There were concerned murmurs as Freddie, 42, arrived at London's exclusive Groucho Club for the bash, but he insisted: "I've never felt better."

And a close friend said: "Some people thought Freddie looked ill, but there is nothing wrong. He really enjoyed himself.

"Freddie has lost a bit of weight, but he needed to, he was getting chubby.

"He always looks a bit anaemic when he's not got his stage make-up on, but he was in a very bubbly mood."

Dozens of Freddie's showbiz mates turned out to help the flamboyant singer celebrate after Queen received a Life-

Before . . . the old Freddie

Continued on Page Five

THE Sun

Wednesday, February 28, 1990   **22p**   Yesterday's estimated sale: 4,010,368   Thought: Caught Knapping

£52,000 LOTTO: Page 9 ● £31,000 BINGO: Page 18

Storm over freed double killer

By **ROBERT JOBSON**

COMMANDO Graham Sherman was **FREED** yesterday after killing his wife and son.

Sherman, 21, blasted 23-year-old Michelle and baby Josh with a shotgun in a fit of depression.

But he walked out of court with just a **TICKING OFF** from 72-year-old Scottish judge Lord Dunpark.

The decision brought outrage from the victim's relatives — and last night two MPs demanded the judge should quit.

Tory Bill Walker said: "He is out of touch with the real world. I wonder if he realises the impact this will have on the community."

Opinion

Scots Nationalist Andrew Welsh said: "I can hardly believe this. I will be asking the Lord Advocate to hold an investigation.

"Lord Dunpark is way out of line as far as public opinion is concerned. It's almost as if the judge decided nothing happened."

The judge had told Sherman: "I'm going to do something I have never done before in a case of culpable homicide and I don't anticipate I will ever do it again.

"I'm going to admonish you on both charges.

"In my opinion, you

Continued on Page Nine

KNAPP OFF

DOOMED ROMANCE   Sherman and Michelle on their wedding day . . . but tragedy lay ahead

NUR boss dumped me says his wife

EXCLUSIVE

RAIL union boss Jimmy Knapp has left his wife after 25 years and is seeing another woman, it was revealed last night.

NUR chief Jimmy, 49, moved out of the house he shared with wife Sylvia.

He now spends much of his time at the home of attractive German brunette Eva Leigh. They often leave together for work from her semi-detached house at West Wickham, Kent.

The break-up has shattered grey-haired Sylvia who is more than ten years older than her husband.

She wept last night and said: "My husband is a

By **ROBERT KELLAWAY**

great man. How could she do this?"

Sylvia added at the family home at Ashford, Kent: "I only found out after my daughter's birthday on January 29. He did not come home until

Continued on Page Four

Jimmy Knapp . . . moved out

Eva . . . German-born

THE Sun

Friday, March 2, 1990   22p   Estimated daily sale for February 3,990,000   Thought: What a hoot

By TREVOR KAVANAGH
Political Editor

A SENIOR Tory has confessed that local authorities **ARE** artificially bumping up poll tax bills.

His admission came as a new poll in today's Daily Telegraph gave Labour an 18.5 per cent lead — their biggest since September, 1971, and three per cent up in a month.

The Tory councillor said: "We cranked up the bills so we could get money to do all those projects we have been putting off for years."

Tory and Labour councils are doing it, he said, because they knew the Government would get blamed over the tax.

Figure

The Tory revealed that his county authority will charge every adult an extra £1.15 a **WEEK** — £60 a year above the figure they could have settled at.

And even that was £40 above the figure the Government had set.

Yet until now, their rate bills had been among the ten **LOWEST**.

He explained: "We could see that the poll tax was hated but the Government, not us, was getting the blame.

"Every county I know has done exactly the same."

Keep your nerve – Page 2
Stuffing our coffers – Page 6

CHAIN GANG

A bike with 13 seats was waiting to be claimed from police at Roath, Cardiff, last night.

CHARLES: WHY I STICK TOOTHPASTE UP MY NOSE..

He nose, y'know . . . Charles with Di yesterday   Pictures ARTHUR EDWARDS

By GUY PATRICK

POTTY Prince Charles revealed yesterday how he stops himself snoring . . . he squirts **TOOTHPASTE** up his nose.

Charles, who often keeps Diana awake with his nightly rumblings, showed how he uses a finger to poke the paste up his hooter.

And he said that if the toothpaste cure didn't work, a **BOILED ONION** eaten before bedtime often did the trick.

The Prince offered his homespun advice to a flood disaster victim evacuated from his home at Towyn, North Wales.

SPICY

Ronald Squire, 53, who is bedding down at a local refuge centre, told Charles he drives his family crazy by snoring "like a train."

Ronald said: "He asked if I had tried putting toothpaste up my nostrils. I said no, and he said he had tried it."

Ronald's wife Brenda,

It stops snores, and so does an onion!

EXCLUSIVE

52, said: "Prince Charles put his fingers towards his nose to demonstrate.

"I said we would give it a go.

"Then he suggested eating a boiled onion before going to bed — and he also mentioned eating plenty of spicy food.

Ronald added: "He was very down to earth. It was like talking to a mate in the pub."

Charles, who is well-known for his love of

Continued on Page Five

£56,000 LOTTO: See Page 18 ● £31,000 BINGO: See Page 20

THE Sun

Friday, 13 April, 1990   22p   Audited daily sale for March: 3,979,395   Thought: Bad Friday

SUN EXCLUSIVE

Marti with Tom . . . so happy   Picture: ADAM PENSOTTI

MARTI, 46 FALLS FOR TOYBOY, 25

By NEIL SYSON and TONY SNOW

SINGER Marti Webb has set up home with a hunky toyboy nearly **HALF** her age. The 46-year-old West End star has fallen for 6ft blond sound engineer Tom Button, 25.

He moved into her £250,000 home last month. Twice-married Marti met Tom in Blackpool last year when they were working on a summer season of hit musical Cats.

Tom was living with actress Lorraine Brunning, 24 — who has appeared in TV's Grange Hill and Home Sweet Home. But he later ditched her and moved in with Marti.

Happy

Yesterday, Marti chuckled when asked about Tom's age and said: "He's old enough!"

Before driving off with Tom in a new Golf GTi from her home in Fulham, West London, Marti added: "We are both very happy together — there's nothing to hide.

"But any talk of marriage is quite ridiculous."

Marti added: "Tom has been living with me since March.

"There is no suggestion I came between him and Lorraine. Their

Continued on Page Three

Vile Viv!

● WEST Indies skipper Viv Richards made V-signs at England supporters **THREE** times yesterday as bitterness erupted at the final Test.

The fans had barracked him for refusing to curb a vicious barrage of bouncers from Windies bowlers.

Full story — Back Page

BLOODY FRENCH SINK OUR HOLS

By EDDIE FITZMAURICE

BLOODY-MINDED French air traffic men will today start to wreck thousands of Britons' Easter holidays in a strike deliberately timed for the busiest weekend of the year so far.

The three-day stoppage — only announced last night — will create havoc as the rush to Mediterranean hot spots gets into full swing.

ALL flights over France will be hit — causing untold misery in packed departure lounges.

British travel agents' spokesman Keith Betton hit out furiously at the French pay strikers.

"They try it on every year," he stormed. "It is a totally heartless gesture by a group of holiday killjoys and causes a massive headache for sunseekers.

QUEUES

"It has become a cheap publicity stunt that we are all rather sick of."

Airport chiefs, faced with moving 700,000 Easter travellers, are dreading a repeat of last year's queues and frustration when holidays were ruined by French air traffic controllers.

At **GATWICK**, which will handle 405,000 passengers this weekend, spokeswoman Jennifer Johnston said: "People should be prepared for the worst.

"I would need a crystal ball to forecast the likely delays."

At **HEATHROW**, 110,000 travellers a day are expected as Britons ignore soaring interest rates and fork out to join the great getaway. Tighter security checks could add to delays.

FLIGHTS

In a further blow, **SPANISH** air traffic controllers grounded some British flights yesterday to ease congestion in their skies.

Today's strike by air traffic planners was ordered by French unions as part of a long-running campaign by aviation staff for more cash and shorter hours.

The planners control aircraft on the ground in France. But their action will disrupt complicated computer routings for flights over the Continent.

Britain's Civil Aviation Authority said last night that routes used by charter flights to Spain and other Mediterranean destinations

Continued on Page Four

THE Sun

Wednesday, May 16, 1990 — 22p — Audited daily sale for April: 3,953,790 — Thought: Stand down Jim

£184,000 **£31,000**

LOTTO: Page Nine — **BINGO:** Page 27

KINNOCK BLOW AS LEFTIES WIN MORE PICKETS

Mr Kinnock . . . won applause

- LABOUR leader Neil Kinnock was dealt a major blow yesterday when Lefties forced through policy changes that could mean a return to mass strike picketing.
- The left-wingers, led by hardline MPs Tony Benn and Dennis Skinner, sabotaged plans to restrict factory pickets to six and decided controls on secondary picketing should be scrapped.
- Bosses fear the decision could mean a return to scenes of mass violence like those outside The Sun's hi-tech plant in Wapping.
- But Mr Kinnock won applause from party managers and trade union bosses when he announced the policies which will form the basis of Labour's general election manifesto.

Full story—Page Two
The Sun Says—Page Six

Gummer . . . meat-eater

Beef is OK for my kids says angry Gummer

By SIMON WALTERS

FARMS Minister John Gummer tried to defuse the "mad cow" panic yesterday — by vowing that his kids would keep eating beef.

He insisted it was safe to serve beef to his children Ben, 12, Felix, eight, Leonora, seven, and four-year-old Cordelia.

Mr Gummer said: "They eat beef, minced beef, beefburgers and beef sausages.

"I would not dream of allowing that or the public to eat beef unless I was absolutely confident."

Advice

Mr Gummer spoke out over the health scare as the number of schools to ban beef rose to nearly 3,000.

Education chiefs in Staffordshire, Bradford, and Richmond, South West London, followed Humberside's lead.

Dorset councils also scrapped beef from hospital menus.

In Oxfordshire a temporary school beef ban starts today while the county council takes expert advice.

Pure beef, burgers, mince and sausages will be taken off school menus.

"It is better to be safe

Continued on Page Two

NICK NICK SACKED SACKED SACKED

Jim . . . blown out over blue jokes

Brawling Jim is stood down by TV bosses

From JIM TAYLOR in Montreux

BRAWLING comic Jim Davidson has had his TV show axed because of his bad-boy antics, The Sun can reveal today.

Fed-up ITV chiefs fear his blue jokes and off-screen fisticuffs are wrecking their image.

The decision to give Nick Nick the chop-chop was made during meetings at the Montreux TV Festival in Switzerland this week.

Executives agreed not to make another series of his one-man show Stand-Up Jim David-

EXCLUSIVE

son, even though it pulls in nine million viewers.

But to fulfil his £300,000 contract, they are pushing ahead with a new series of his other show, Home James.

PUSHING

Trouble has been Jim's middle name this year after:

POLICE were called to a punch-up at his home which left his children's nanny with a bruised jaw;

He **BRAWLED** at a hotel with an actor in a row over the Falklands War;

COMPLAINTS from hundreds of TV viewers about his racist and sexist jokes.

AXING of dozens of his gags which were too crude even for a late-night adult time slot.

One Thames executive said last night: "Enough is enough.

"There is no doubt that Jim is bursting with talent.

"But we knew it would be a gamble when we agreed to give him the chance to try his late-night risqué stuff on TV.

"We were prepared for the critics but we did not expect Jim to go off the rails in his private life.

"He wants desperately to be liked but under pressure he can

Continued on Page Three

THE Sun

Friday, May 25, 1990   **22p**   Audited daily sale for April: 3,953,790   Thought: What a send off

WORLD CUP WALLIES

Gazza quizzed by cops

after bust-up outside a bar

By GUY PATRICK

SOCCER ace Paul Gascoigne has been quizzed over a bust-up as he prepared to join England's World Cup squad.

The Spurs midfielder was involved in a clash outside a wine bar.

Geordie Gazza, 22, was visiting his family and girlfriend Gail Pringle on Tyneside before flying to Italy today with the other England players.

He and Gail were on their way to Newcastle's swish Berlin's bar when a heated exchange took place with a man.

Police last night confirmed that graduate Anthony Marshall, 31, had accused Gascoigne of attacking him.

REPORT

A spokesman said: "He was released without being charged and a report will be sent to the Crown Prosecution Service."

Gascoigne, who went to the police voluntarily, refused to comment as he arrived at the England squad's Luton hotel last night.

Gascoigne . . . wine-bar row

Robson yesterday . . . "I wanted to do it properly, that is all gone"

England in turmoil as boss Robson admits: I quit

ENGLAND'S World Cup plans were in chaos last night after manager Bobby Robson revealed that he IS quitting.

But he was furious that his plans to take over as £250,000-a-year boss of Dutch club PSV Eindhoven were revealed before the finals.

He wanted to keep the move a secret until he had broken it to his players next week at their World Cup HQ in Italy.

Instead the news was forced out by claims that he had quit because ex-lover Janet Rush was publishing a book telling of their five-year affair.

CHARGE

Robson said the publicity had caused "an absolute bombshell."

He said: "I wanted to do it quietly and properly.

"We were going to take proper steps with the players, but that is all gone now."

Robson added: "It has come at a very untimely moment when we were

By TONY SNOW

going abroad to play in the World Cup with morale good and with me in charge, and nothing else to do but attempt to win the Cup with a decent bunch of players.

"That has been ruined with a flimsy story. I find that appalling."

Robson said he had never offered to resign—and would certainly not quit because of the Janet Rush book.

He said: "It's by an ex-girlfriend. All that happened 13 years ago."

EX-MISTRESS SPEAKS: Pages 4 & 5 ● SUNSPORT SPECIAL: Pages 36, 37, 38, 39 & 40

THE Sun

Sun showbiz special

HOW MADONNA FLIRTED HER WAY TO FAME

MADONNA . . . sexy games

CENTRE PAGES

Tuesday, July 17, 1990   22p   Audited daily sale for June 3,892,098   Thought: Oompah strikes back

LAGER KRAUTS

Another **Sun** exclusive

EXCLUSIVE

MORE MISERY FROM MAJOR

No tax cuts and no home loan relief

By DAVID KEMP

CHANCELLOR John Major will tell the Cabinet this week there will be **NO** tax cuts in his Budget next spring.

And there will be **NO** reduction in interest rates before the end of this year.

At a Downing Street meeting on Thursday he will admit the economy has not improved as fast as he would have liked.

Hopes of keeping inflation under 10 per cent have also been dashed.

The blows come despite figures yesterday showing retail sales down 2.8 per cent last month — the biggest fall in shop business for 11 years.

Ceiling

Mr Major had hoped his next Budget would be a vote-winning package of modest tax cuts and low inflation.

He also wanted to help hard-pressed home-buyers by cutting interest rates and raising the ceiling on mortgage tax relief from £30,000 to £40,000.

On the inflation front, Mr Major is now resigned to seeing price rises crash through the 10 per cent barrier in the next few months.

It should then drop. But Mr Major will tell the Cabinet he won't be able to achieve his 7.5 per cent target by the end of the year — it will still be 9 per cent or above.

Mrs Thatcher hopes to go for a historic fourth election victory next autumn.

But some Ministers believe
Continued on Page Two

£108,000
LOTTO - Page 4

£31,000
BINGO - Page 21

Together . . . the loving couple before glamour girl Patsy's movie career rocketed

By PIERS MORGAN

● HOLLYWOOD golden girl Patsy Kensit, the 22-year-old star of Absolute Beginners and Lethal Weapon II, has split from husband Dan Donovan.

● The couple's two-year marriage crumbled as Patsy's success left Dan, 27 — keyboard player with rock group Big Audio Dynamite — trailing behind.

● A spokesman for the pair said: "They have separated but do not wish to say anything else. It was just a case of two people drifting apart."

I thought I'd be Mrs Donovan for ever — Page Nine

PATSY'S PARTING

● MP protests at Sieg Heil rumpus
● Oompah band tolled bells at 2am

BOOZY Germans lived up to Nicholas Ridley's worst fears when they invaded an English village, it was revealed last night.

The lager Krauts, in a visiting fire brigade brass band, upset residents when they:
● **TOLLED** church bells at 2am;
● **SHOUTED** "Sieg Heil" and sang their wartime national anthem;
● **FLEW** a German flag above the cricket pavilion;
● **KEPT** villagers awake with their singing and oompahs.

By ANDY LINES

SYMPATHY

As the strains of Deutschland Uber Alles (Germany Over All) rang out in the night air, **THREE** brassed-off Brits called the police, including Tory MP Jerry Hayes.

Mr Hayes, whose home overlooks the cricket pitch in Wendens Ambo, near Saffron Walden, Essex, stormed: "I almost had sympathy for Nicholas Ridley's views on the Germans.

"There was a hell of a row going on. They were singing and playing from about 11pm.

"And then the church bells started ringing.

"I could hear the German national anthem being played, several
Continued on Page Seven

THE Sun

Thursday, August 9, 1990   22p   Audited daily sale for June 3,892,098   Thought: We're with you, buddy

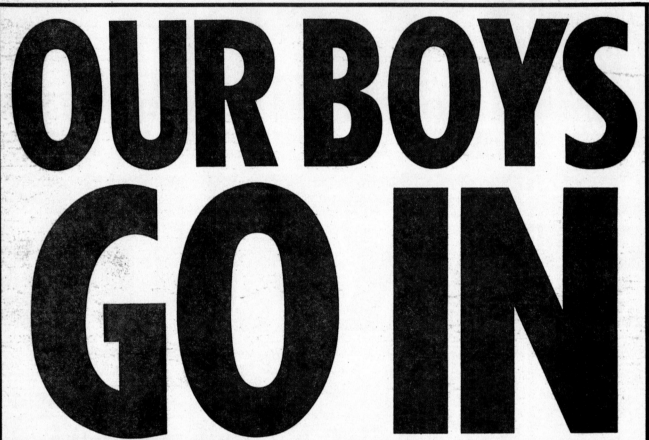

OUR BOYS GO IN

● Paras to take on madman
● Ships, planes on their way

MRS Thatcher yesterday ordered crack British troops and RAF jet fighters into the Gulf to back America's bid to smash Iraqi tyrant Saddam Hussein.

The order went out after a meeting of the War Cabinet in Downing Street.

According to a top Cabinet source, Britain is ready to send **MORE** troops in "on the

By TREVOR KAVANAGH
Political Editor

ground" alongside American Marines if necessary to drive the Iraqis out of Kuwait.

In a massive show of strength unrivalled since the Falklands War, Britain is fielding:

Tornado F3 1,500-mph interceptors, already secretly flown out to Bahrain, Oman and Jeddah, to join a squadron of 12 in Cyprus.

Tornado GR1 fighter-

bomber variants, **Jaguar** fighters and **Harrier** jump jets.

Accompanying them will be **VC-10** tankers for in-flight refuelling.

SUPPORT

And they will get back-up, if necessary, from crack paras of the **5th Airborne Brigade**, based in Aldershot, the elite **SAS** — already in Cyprus — and its naval counterpart the **Special Boat Service**.

All leave has been cancelled and only a skeleton force

from these rapid-deployment units will remain in Britain.

Airmen serving in the **RAF Rapier Regiment** at Abingdon, Oxfordshire, and at Lyneham, Wilts, have been recalled from leave.

The regiment is trained in guided-missile defence systems, including the use of nuclear weapons, and would be deployed to protect British fighter squadrons.

The 5th Airborne Brigade includes the 1st and 2nd Bat-

Continued on Page Three

THE WAR THREAT GROWS—Pages 2, 3, 4, 5 and 6

THE Sun

Tuesday, August 14, 1990   22p   Audited daily sale for July 3,839,519   Thought: Core blimey

5 airgirls raped in Iraqi raid on hostel

By SUN FOREIGN DESK

AN air hostess told last night how she saw **FIVE** other stewardesses — including two British girls — gang-raped at gunpoint by Iraqi troops.

Nawal Bel Hadj said eight soldiers armed with machine guns stormed into the lobby of a Kuwait hostel where the air girls were staying.

She said: "They told our Indian servant, 'Get us women, we need women.'

"We were in our rooms listening to them. Then other stewardesses, not knowing what was happening, came down in the lift to the lobby.

Fled

"As soon as they opened the door of the lift the soldiers grabbed them.

"They made a circle around the girls and then attacked them."

Her voice choking with emotion, 24-year-old Nawal went on: "The girls were crying...we could not save them...we fled through the back door.

"The Iraqi soldiers were like crazy, rabid dogs. These people had never seen women in their lives.

Savages

"They are savages. I will never forget these atrocities."

None of the raped hostesses — the two Britons, two Egyptians and a Filipino — have been seen since the attack, which happened five days after Iraqi troops invaded Kuwait.

The air girls who escaped the hostel hid in nearby flats.

Tunisian Nawal was among 3,000 Arabs who crossed the border into Jordan yesterday.

GET IT DOWN!

Workmen demolishing a Manchester building swigged two bottles of 1900 champagne and three of 1881 brandy worth £5,000 found in the ruins.

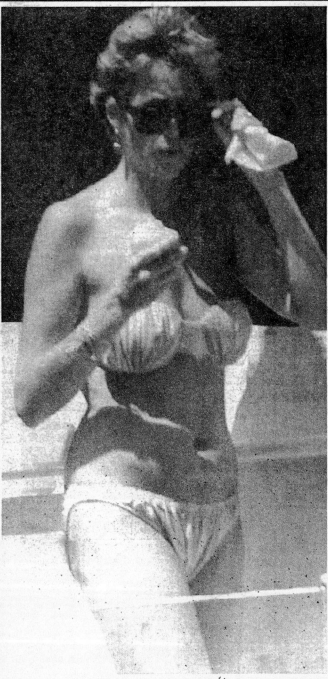

Apple and dream . . . Di has a sunshine snack   Picture: ARTHUR EDWARDS

ITSY BITSY, TEENY WEENY, DI'S A DREAM IN HER BIKINI

From PHIL DAMPIER in Majorca

PRINCESS Di looked a sunshine stunner yesterday as she relaxed in the TEENIEST of bikinis.

Smiling Di donned the itsy-bitsy red number to make the most of the Mediterranean heat.

She lounged with Prince Charles on the deck of Spanish King Juan Carlos's £6million yacht Fortuna off Majorca.

Di was lapping up every moment of the couple's summer break.

She giggled as she sat next to her husband, eating an apple. Charles — still in pain after breaking his right arm playing polo — seemed less at ease.

Two years ago, he romped on the beach and played sandcastles with sons William and Harry.

PLASTER

But yesterday he gazed longingly at the sea, knowing he could not take a cooling dip because of his plaster cast.

Di has worn her teeny weeny bikini — a £53 Gottex

Continued on Page Three

THE Sun

Wednesday, September 26, 1990   **22p**   Audited daily sale for August: 3,883,871   Thought: Pay up now

THE DESERT PRATS

Singer George . . . bare bottoms banned from ad

GEORGE'S NUDE AD CENSORED

By PIERS MORGAN

SUPERSTAR George Michael's telly advert for his new album has been **CENSORED** because it was too raunchy.

The 60-second commercial, which George directed, originally featured a man and a woman **STRIPPING** off, **FONDLING** each other and standing **NAKED** with their backs to the camera. But TV watchdogs from the Independent Broadcasting Authority told the rock star the ad was too explicit.

Tonight, viewers will see an edited version showing only the couple's backs naked from the waist **UP**.

Proud

An IBA spokesman said last night: "Nudity is not allowed unless it is within the context of the advertised product."

A spokesman for George, 27, said: "He was very proud of the advert. It was intended to give a clear interpretation of his album."

The cheeky ad, which plugs George's No. 1 album Listen Without Prejudice, has been shown in America and Australia.

£3m FINE FOR SICK SIR JACK

SICK financier Sir Jack Lyons was fined £3million yesterday for his part in the Guinness shares scandal — but escaped jail.

Southwark Crown Court heard that a prison term could kill Lyons, 74, a friend of Mrs Thatcher.

Mr Justice Henry spared Lyons from a 2½-year sentence because the tycoon has cancer of the bladder and bronchitis.

Sir Jock to lose knighthood — Page 7

£230,000 LOTTO: Page 12
£31,000 BINGO: Page 21

GIs pay is up £90 a month

Frog troops paid double

Aussie cash up £20 a day

Belgians get 100% rise

But we CUT £85 a month

The Sun says

LOOK carefully at the figures on the left.

They tell an outrageous story of how the Government are trying to get courage and sacrifice on the cheap.

Every Western country with forces in the Gulf is giving its men extra pay and allowances.

Every country, that is, except Britain.

Our boys are having their pay **CUT**.

The grinding, flint-hearted officials in the Defence Ministry got out their money ledgers.

Disgraceful

They reckoned that the cost of living was higher in West Germany, where the 7,000 soldiers of the Desert Rats Armoured Brigade are based, than it would be in the Middle East.

After all, when men were in the front line, there would be fewer opportunities to go shopping.

Incredibly, the bureaucrats are **SLASHING** up to £85 a month off

Continued on Page Two

THE Sun

Wednesday, October 10, 1990 **25p** Est daily sale September 3,970,213 Thought: British Bust Corporation

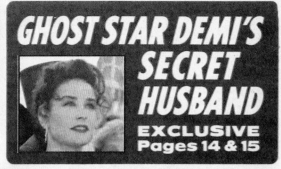

GHOST STAR DEMI'S SECRET HUSBAND
EXCLUSIVE Pages 14 & 15

Waite . . . close to freedom

Waite to be freed tomorrow say Arabs

By NICK PARKER

HOSTAGE Terry Waite will be released **TOMORROW**, senior Arab sources said last night.

His fellow British captive John McCarthy is due to be freed at the same time.

Church envoy Waite, 51, and journalist McCarthy, 33, have been given new clothes ready for their reappearance in the world tomorrow evening.

A third hostage, believed to be 76-year-old former Battle of Britain pilot Jackie Mann, may also go free.

Mission

News that Waite and McCarthy's nightmare was about to end came in an influential Lebanese newspaper.

The paper correctly predicted the release dates of Irish hostage Brian Keenan and American Frank Reid.

It is now known all three hostages have been held in the Hizbollah stronghold of Baalbeck 50 miles east of Beirut.

They are due to be released in the Syrian capital Damascus before being flown home.

A diplomatic source in Damascus said last night: "They can expect to be on their way home by Thursday night."

WOT NO SAND!

Squaddies filling sandbags on the desert island air base of Muharraq in the Gulf have worked so hard they have run out of **SAND!**

NEW BOOBS ON THE BEEB

BEFORE *Trim beauty Cindy Jackson the way she used to appear*

AFTER *Cindy shapes up nicely thanks to the extra inches provided by top surgeon*

Cindy gets £1,500 for breast op

EXCLUSIVE

By MARTIN DUNN

THE BBC has spent £1,500 to give a former model bigger boobs, it was revealed last night.

Cindy Jackson, 27, had her breasts enlarged by two inches for a TV show.

The op was carried out by a top surgeon in Knightsbridge, West London.

BBC chiefs faced a storm of protest last night as MPs accused them of wasting licence payers' money.

Cindy said producers of the Ruby Wax Show paid for the surgery last month.

CHEQUE

She said: "They wanted to do a piece on someone undergoing breast enlargement.

"They wanted to follow someone through the operation, talking to them before and afterwards.

"They knew I had had plastic surgery. I told them I wasn't planning to have the operation because I couldn't afford it.

"They said they would pick up the £1,500 bill."

A cheque drawn on the BBC Accounting Services Television ac-

Continued on Page Two

£254,000 LOTTO: Page 21 ● **£31,000 BINGO: Page 24** ● **Colour Code Page 28**

Sun SPORT

Wednesday, October 10, 1990 ☆ ☆ ☆ ☆

8 PAGES OF SUNSPORT

BANGER 'N' BASH

KOP hero Ian Rush scored a hat-trick to notch up 251 goals for Liverpool on the night a raw kid thumped home three on his first-team debut.

Rushy's goals, his 249th, 250th and 251st for the Anfield giants swamped Crewe, who were battered 4-1 and went down 9-2 on ag-gregate in the Rumbelows Cup.

Rushy's an old hand at scoring, but 19-year-old Southampton striker Nicky Banger showed his own lethal touch.

He belted in a hat-trick at Rochdale lost 3-0 on the night and 8-0 on aggregate.

Banger, who had scored eight in six games in the reserves, played only because star forwards Matthew Le Tissier and Rod Wallace were rested.

And another master blaster was Everton's Graeme Sharp, who also crashed home a hat-trick as Wrexham went down 6-0 — that's 11-0 on aggregate.

LATE NIGHT ACTION SPECIAL

GOAL . . . Paul Merson celebrates   Picture: RICHARD PELHAM

STICK IT UP YOUR LIMPAR!

Perry's just as Swede

By BRIAN WOOLNOUGH: Arsenal 5 Chester 0 (Arsenal win 6-0 on agg)

PERRY GROVES last night blasted out a two-goal message to walk-out rebel Anders Limpar: You won't be missed!

Groves stepped into the Arsenal line-up for the absent Swede in this Rumbelows Cup clash at Highbury.

And with Limpar in Stockholm — where he is preparing for Sweden's match against Germany tonight — Groves took full advantage.

His first-half double not only knocked the stuffing out of Chester, it left Limpar facing a battle for his place when he returns.

Groves had a transfer request turned down last month and Gunners boss George Graham confirmed: "Perry emphasised why I can't let him go. I need a strong squad."

Alan Smith, Tony Adams and Paul Merson also got on the scoresheet as Arsenal booked their place in the third round and Graham added:

"It was good to get five and with Adams scoring that's nine players this season who have found the net.

"But I expected more. Had we seen a real ruthless edge, it could have been ten."

Poor Chester just couldn't cope from the moment Groves struck in the 10th minute with a brave header from Lee Dixon's cross.

Confused

Fifteen minutes later, Groves made it 2-0, coolly turning in David Rocastle's deep pass from the right.

A third goal was inev-itable and it came five minutes before half-time when Smith headed in after Dixon and Merson had confused the Third Division side.

Lucky

It was just a question of how many Arsenal would score and their fourth came from skip-per Adams — though the England international was lucky to be on the field when he pounced in the 67th minute.

Five minutes earlier, Adams had been booked for a late challenge on Carl Dale and minutes later upended the Ches-ter striker with a blatant

ANDERS LIMPAR

Anders OK says George

GEORGE GRAHAM last night promised Swedish rebel Anders Limpar: I won't give you a roast-ing when you return.

The Arsenal boss said: "There will be no disci-plinary action.

"Nothing has changed about that situation. He has passed a medical in Sweden and whether he plays we'll have to see."

Earlier the Swedish FA snubbed Graham's de-mand that they should take out £1.5m insurance cover on Limpar in case he was permanently crocked in tonight's match against Germany.

● Turn to Page 39

HAGAR THE HORRIBLE   By CHRIS BROWNE

SAVE THE DRAGONS

SAVE THE DRAGONS

CARE TO CONTRIBUTE TO OUR CAMPAIGN TO SAVE THE DRAGONS?

SOME OTHER TIME PERHAPS

THE Sun

Tuesday, October 30, 1990   25p   Audited daily sale for September 3,979,330   Thought: Goal-den boy

TOP COP IMBERT IN HEART DRAMA

By JOHN MURPHY

BRITAIN'S top cop Sir Peter Imbert was in intensive care last night after a suspected heart attack.

The Metropolitan Police Commissioner's condition was at first said to be "comfortable."

But a specialist was later called from home to examine him after it was believed he had deteriorated.

Sir Peter, 57, felt unwell after horse-riding in London's Hyde Park.

He was being driven back to New Scotland Yard

Continued on Page Two

Sir Peter . . . pressure

Clowning Street . . . joker Gazza puts his arm round Maggie's shoulders at a No 10 party. 'She's nice and cuddly,' he says

GAZZA MEETS MAGGA

By NEIL SYSON

SOCCER star Paul Gascoigne hugged Mrs Thatcher last night and joked: "I'm taking her out for a drink."

Gazza, 23, turned Maggie's den into 10 Clowning Street as the Prime Minister greeted him with a handshake at a reception.

The World Cup hero put his arm around her and declared: "She is nice and cuddly."

Gazza — dressed in an

Continued on Page Three

THE Sun

Thursday, November 1, 1990   **25p**   Audited daily sale for September 3,979,330   Thought: Jaques-ass

UP YOURS DELORS

At midday tomorrow Sun readers are urged to tell the French fool where to stuff his ECU

By NICK PARKER, PETE WALSH and LIZ DUXBURY
(Sun Diplomatic Staff)

THE Sun today calls on its patriotic family of readers to tell the feelthy French to FROG OFF!

They **INSULT** us, **BURN** our lambs, **FLOOD** our country with dodgy food and **PLOT** to abolish the dear old pound.

Now it's your turn to kick **THEM** *in the Gauls.*

We want you to tell Froggie Common Market chief Jacques Delors exactly what you think of him and his countrymen.

At the stroke of noon tomorrow, we invite all true blue Brits to face France and yell "Up Yours, Delors."

The ear-bashing from our millions of readers will wake the EC President up to the fact that he will **NEVER** run our country.

His bid to replace the £ with the faceless ECU is the last straw after centuries of Froggy Brit-baiting. They **BURNED** alive British lambs earlier this year because they couldn't match our quality. They also:

JEERED Mrs Thatcher when she visited Paris to boost celebrations for the bi-centenary of the French Revolution last year;

FOUL

BANNED British beef after falsely claiming it had mad cow disease;

BLEATED when we found their foul soft cheese was riddled with listeria bugs;

GAVE IN to the Nazis during the Second World War when we stood firm;

TRIED to conquer Europe until we put down Napoleon at Waterloo in 1815 and

Remember, folks, it won't be long before the garlic-breathed bastilles will be here in droves once the Channel Tunnel is open.

So grab your megaphones, turn south and let 'em hear the British lion **ROAR**.

And the best of British to you all!

Where to bowl at the Gauls — Pages 2 and 3

THE Sun

Wednesday, November 21, 1990   **25p**   Audited daily sale for October 3,929,810   Thought: Four short

204

SO CLOSE TO VICTORY

Defiant Premier Mrs Thatcher . . . an outright win in the first leadership ballot just eluded her last night

MAGGIE

152

TARZAN

I fight on vows PM as she misses by 4 votes

PREMIER Margaret Thatcher pledged a fight to the death with Tory leadership challenger Michael Heseltine last night.

She vowed to enter a second-round battle after falling just **FOUR VOTES** short of the 56 majority she needed to destroy his bid outright.

The Prime Minister scored 204 against 152 for Tarzan. There were 16 abstentions.

MPs who expected her to take the hint and quit were stunned when she announced within minutes of the result "I'm fighting on."

Some Tory MPs believe Mrs Thatcher is now damaged goods and

By TREVOR KAVANAGH and SIMON WALTERS

have already warned party managers they will defect in the next round.

Others said they voted for Mr Heseltine only to give Mrs Thatcher a short, sharp shock and Continued on Page Two

Heseltine . . . Round 2 fight

THE **S**un

Wednesday, November 28, 1990   **25p**   Audited sale for October 3,929,810   Thought: King John

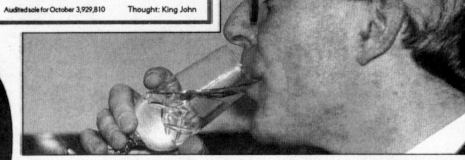

Bubbling spirits . . . a champagne toast from John Major as he becomes Britain's new Premier

PREMIER **M**AJOR

By TREVOR KAVANAGH
Political Editor

JOHN MAJOR is Britain's new Prime Minister after thrashing Michael Heseltine in last night's Tory leadership vote.

Chancellor Mr Major, 47, who only joined the Cabinet three years ago, scored 185 votes to Mr Heseltine's 131.

Foreign Secretary Douglas Hurd trailed in third with 56.

Last night Mr Major publicly thanked his rivals for their conduct during the contest. He told Tory MPs: "I want a Cabinet of all their talents" — hinting at a top job for Mr Heseltine.

Mr Major's vote tally was actually **TWO SHORT** of the 187 he needed for outright victory in the second ballot.

But both Mr Heseltine and Mr Hurd immediately pulled out of the fight, making a third ballot unnecessary.

PRESSURE

Mrs Thatcher, spending her last day at No 10, said she was "thrilled" by her protege's triumph.

Then she went next door to No 11, hugged Mr Major and congratulated him.

On the doorstep, Mr Major said the Tory Party's job was now clear.

"We are going to unite, we are going to unite totally and absolutely and we are going to win the next General Election," he declared.

Mr Major, who was brought up in rented rooms in Brixton,

Continued on Page Two

● **He crushes Heseltine**

● **Maggie cuddles him**

PREMIER MAJOR — SEE PAGES 2, 3, 4, 5 and 6 PLUS FOUR-PAGE PULLOUT

THE Sun

Saturday, December 22, 1990   25p   Audited sale for November 3,817,382   Thought: Court out

SONIA BIKE

Sonia . . . rocked in her seat

Ripper's wife faces ruin
and £300,000 libel bill

YORKSHIRE Ripper's wife Sonia Sutcliffe faced ruin last night after LOSING her libel case against the News Of The World.

Sonia, 40, was ordered to pay **ALL** the £300,000 costs of the 15-day High Court case. It virtually wiped out the £334,000 she piled up from eight court victories against newspapers in seven years.

And Private Eye magazine, ordered to pay Sonia £160,000 last year, announced that it would seek fresh court action in the light of allegations that she perjured herself in evidence against them. That could cost Sonia **ANOTHER** £200,000 in costs.

Sonia, thought to be worth around £230,000, faces bankruptcy **AND** losing her £100,000 house in Bradford.

As the jury announced its verdict in the News Of The World case, she rocked backwards and forwards in her seat, grim-faced, her lips pressed tightly together.

Mr Justice Drake ruled that £150,000 of her cash could not be moved without giving News Of The World solicitors seven days notice.

Mr George Carman QC, for the newspaper, said there was concern that the assets should not be dissipated or removed abroad. News Of

By TONY SNOW

The World legal boss Tom Crone called the verdict "a victory for fairness and common sense."

He said of Sonia: "She has only her own greed to blame. We trust this means her gravy train has finally hit the buffers.

"We hope this is a clear message to all those other avaricious people out there who think they can take newspapers and libel juries for a ride."

DOCUMENTS

After the case, Sonia's lawyer said: "She has no comment to make."

Private Eye lawyers were last night studying the evidence.

Sonia won £100,000 and £600,000 from the magazine — later reduced *Continued on Page Two*

THE SUN SAYS
The liar loses

SONIA SUTCLIFFE loses and so do liars everywhere.

It is a victory for all newspapers whose duty is to ferret out and publish the truth.

The jury Sonia Sutcliffe failed to fool also deserve credit for vindicating and protecting freedom of speech.

SEE PAGE 6

£380,000 LOTTO: Page 9 ● £31,000 BINGO: Page 19

Thursday, December 27, 1990   25p   Audited sale for November 3,817,382   Thought: Bagged cad

You take my breath away . . . heart-throb Cruise and actress bride Nicole

Top Gun Tom weds

By ANDY COULSON
Showbusiness Reporter

TOP GUN star Tom Cruise secretly wed his lover Nicole Kidman on Christmas Eve, it was revealed last night.

Hollywood heart-throb Cruise married the 23-year-old Aussie actress in the millionaires' ski resort of Aspen, Colorado.

Just **TEN** relatives were at the wedding — which was so hush-hush that even Nicole's uncle and aunt were kept in the dark.

Cruise, 28 — who divorced his first wife, U.S. actress Mimi Rogers, earlier this year — had

SECRET 'I DO' FOR NICOLE

ordered both sets of parents to keep the wedding under wraps.

Romantic

Last night, Nicole's uncle Barry Fawcett said: "We had no idea about the marriage."

All he and wife Linda knew was that Nicole's parents Tony and Janelle were spending Christ-

mas in America. Linda revealed: "Tony told us Tom and Nicole didn't want the wedding to turn into a circus.

"It was extremely well planned because nobody knew about it until afterwards."

Nicole's mum and dad jetted to Aspen last week to prepare for the wedding. The actress's younger sister Antonia was bridesmaid at the 30-minute civil ceremony.

Speaking at the family home in Sydney, Barry added: "Tom and Nicole wanted a romantic ceremony without any fuss. There

Continued on Page Three

Dessie . . . favourite

DESSIE IS BETTA THAN GAZZA!

By MICHAEL FIELDER

WONDER horse Desert Orchid scored a Boxing Day record — with footwork to rival Gazza's. Dessie notched up a **FOURTH** win in the King George VI Chase after neatly side-stepping fallen Sabin du Loir.

Rider Richard Dunwoody said after the 9-4 favourite's Kempton victory: "He nipped round the fallen horse better than Paul Gascoigne."

Now Dessie will try for a second Cheltenham Gold Cup win.

Full story — Page 42

BYE, BYE BAGHDAD

Saddam . . . capital would be razed in "Hiroshima" strike

ISRAEL will wipe out Baghdad with nuclear weapons if Saddam Hussein launches an Iraqi attack on them.

The knockout blow will come **BEFORE** Saddam can carry out his threat to "scorch" Israel, it was revealed last night.

Missiles which Saddam would use to rain deadly poison gas take at least an hour to load up.

By DAVID WOODING

Highly-placed Israeli sources say their spy satellites will give them warning before this can be completed.

BUNKERS

The moment they detect Iraqi missiles being prepared for action, atomic weapons will be dropped on a live target for the first time since World War Two.

Israel has ample firepower to flatten the

Iraqi capital in retaliation, just as the Japanese city of Hiroshima was devastated 45 years ago.

But at first, the Israelis will probably go for selective strikes against Saddam's bunkers and key military posts.

Even a limited blitz would kill hundreds of thousands of Baghdad's five million population and condemn many more to slow death.

Military experts fear such an attack would unite Arab states against

Continued on Page Two

Israel to nuke Saddam if he loads missiles

£386,000 LOTTO: See Page 18 ● £31,000   BINGO: See Page 38

THE Sun

Wednesday, January 16, 1991 **25p** Estimated sale yesterday 3,803,129 Thought: Come home soon

SUPPORT OUR BOYS AND PUT THIS FLAG IN YOUR WINDOW

MAJOR: BACK OUR LADS - PAGES 2 & 3 ● IF WE DIE, WE DIE! - PAGES 4 & 5 ● IRAQ AND RUIN - PAGE 7

THE Sun

Thursday, January 17, 1991   **25p**   Estimated sale yesterday 3,805,247   Thought: God speed

8 a.m. war news

WIPE OUT

- **Iraq's atom base blitzed**
- **Baghdad hit by missiles**

From NICK PARKER and TREVOR KAVANAGH
in the Gulf

EVIL Saddam Hussein was staring defeat in the face early today after a devastating aerial bombardment on Iraq by the Allies.

An atomic weapons plant outside Baghdad was among the first targets wiped out in a barrage of cruise missiles.

Allied jets knocked out nearly all Iraq's 100 airfields and batteries of deadly Scud missiles pointing at Israel were blasted out of sight

Continued on Page Two

WAR SPECIAL: See Pages 2, 3, 4, 5, 6, 7, 9 and 13

THE Sun

2 P.M.

Thursday, January 17, 1991 **25p** Estimated sale yesterday 3,805,247 Thought: Hussein sorry now

AFTERNOON WAR EDITION

BIGGEST AIR RAID EVER

- **18,000 tons of bombs blitz Iraq**
- **RAF Tornado lost in daylight raid**

WAR LATEST: See Pages 2, 3, 4, 5, 6, 7, 9, 13 and BACK PAGE

THE Sun

PAPER THAT BACKS OUR BOYS AND GIRLS

Tuesday, January 22, 1991 **25p** Estimated daily sale last week 3,835,274   Thought: Don't despair, lads, we're all with you

Saddam . . . evil monster

BASTARDS OF BAGHDAD

Hang Saddam long and slow

PAGE ONE OPINION

THE faces of captured British airmen Adrian Nichol and John Peters will haunt us all for many a long day.

So brave when they went into battle, so helpless when captors paraded them on television.

Adrian's mumbled and hollow words, like those of the two American fliers with him, were obviously **DICTATED** by an Iraqi propaganda writer.

How they must have stuck in his throat as he was forced, under what threats we dare not even imagine, to denounce the Allied mission in which he had played such a gallant part.

No one can believe the sentiments uttered by Flight Lieutenant Nichol, in a voice drained of emotion, were his own.

They were the words of an evil monster, Saddam Hussein, and the Bastards of Baghdad.

Our thoughts and our compas-

Terror . . . the haunted face of Adrian Nichol on Iraqi TV

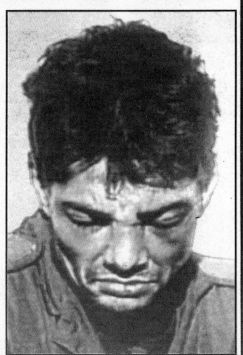

Terror . . . battered John Peters who defied Saddam's thugs

Continued on Page Six

GULF WAR LATEST: See Pages 2, 3, 4, 5, 6, 7, 9, 11 and 12

THE Sun

Thursday, January 24, 1991   **25p**   Estimated daily sale last week 3,835,274   In our thoughts today: Robert Stewart, facing hell in Iraq

PATRIOTS 4
SCUDS...0

Saddam rockets
blown out of sky

From **NEIL SYSON** In Tel Aviv

THE fabulous Patriot missile scored another stunning success over Saddam Hussein's Scuds last night.

Iraq unleashed a wave of Scud attacks on two countries — but all four rockets hurtling in to the three cities were destroyed before they could do any harm.

MISSILE ONE homed in on Tel Aviv, Israel. But a single Patriot was launched — and obliterated the Scud.

MISSILES TWO and **THREE** were fired at the fortress city of Dhahran in eastern Saudi Arabia.

MOBILE

Four Patriots — costing £500,000 apiece — were sent up.

Two huge explosions told witnesses the Scuds had been blasted out of the sky.

MISSILE FOUR, fired as part of a simultaneous salvo, threatened to smash into the Saudi capital of Riyadh.

An unerring Patriot put paid to that Scud as

Continued on Page Two

RAF MAN GRABBED

A THIRD British flier has been captured by the Iraqis after baling out of his stricken Tornado jet, it was revealed last night.

Flight Lieutenant Robert Stewart, a father of two, was navigator in the third Tornado to vanish.

Defence chiefs fear Stewart, 44, will now be paraded on Iraq TV.

The RAF always believed Stewart and pilot David Waddington, 24, survived the crash. Signals from their locators were briefly monitored

Continued on Page Nine

Flashpoint . . . a U.S. Patriot missile blows up an Iraqi Scud rocket fired at Allied forces in Dhahran, Saudi Arabia last night

Inside today   **Sun SLIMMING**   **TRIM-ENDOUS 12-PAGE ALL-STAR PULLOUT!**

THE Sun

25p

WE BACK OUR HEROES

Tuesday, January 29, 1991   25p   Estimated daily sale last week 3,777,831   In our thoughts today: Pte Ronnie Pryde; L Cpl Tracey Ann Morton; Sgt Gary Stunell

Saddam . . . exodus

CAUGHT WITH HIS FLIERS DOWN

From TREVOR KAVANAGH in Riyadh and SIMON HUGHES in London

AT LEAST 100 Iraqi warplanes had fled to the shelter of Iran last night — giving the Allies total control of the Gulf skies.

Military experts claimed Saddam Hussein **ORDERED** the mass exodus to save his deadliest jets from destruction.

The tyrant realises "the game is up," said one senior British source.

And early today in a TV interview, Saddam warned he may arm a Scud with a nuclear warhead if his losses became too great. He knows he faces humiliating defeat and wants to preserve the best of his air force to give him a power base **AFTER** the war.

The aircraft were last night said to be escaping over the border "in entire squadrons."

That allowed Allied fighters to fly with impunity over southern Iraq to protect bombers smashing ground forces and key targets.

RAF Group Captain Niall Irving said at Allied Command HQ in the Saudi capital of Riyadh: "We have moved from air superiority to air supremacy.

MOVE

"The extent to which Iraq can operate is hardly worth talking about."

Saddam now has fewer than 600 aircraft left in Iraq.

Neutral Iran last night repeated that any planes landing in its territory will be held until the end of the conflict.

Its ambassador to Abu Dhabi said the Iraqi planes were being held for "humanitarian" reasons.

It is believed all were unarmed, and have been disabled by Iranian engineers.

Allied experts said

● Saddam sends 100 jets to Iran

Saddam's extraordinary tactics showed a "callous disregard" for his ground forces, who are under constant air bombardment.

One expert said: "He is trying to conserve his assets for the future by sending them out of the way to Iran.

"When the Allied forces switched from attacking runways to pin-point raids on the doors of his underground aircraft bunkers, he knew he had to move the planes or lose them.

"He knows no government will ever again sell him Mirages or MiGs, and that the UN may place an arms em-

● He threatens a nuke last throw

bargo on him. To save his planes, he has left his troops without any air cover.

"And B52 bombers are pounding his Republican Guards with 1,000lb and 2,000lb bombs at the rate of one every 45 seconds."

Many of the aircraft sent to neighbouring

Iran were Saddam's most advanced — the Mirage F-1, Su-24 Fencer, MiG-29 Fulcrum and MiG-23 Flogger.

Some are the only Iraqi warplanes capable of taking on America's mighty F-14 Tomcats and F-15 Eagles.

Two of Iraq's three Adnan early-warning

Continued on Page Two

DAVID PLATT

mita copiers

THE Sun

THE PAPER
THAT SUPPORTS
OUR BOYS
AND GIRLS

Saturday, February 16, 1991   **25p**   Audited daily sale for January 3,742,454   Thought: No peace for the wicked

SADDAM THE SHAM

IT'S SHEDDED BLISS! MADDY LOSES A STONE

By PIERS MORGAN and ROBERT JOBSON

COMPOSER Andrew Lloyd Webber's bride unveiled her fabulous new slimline figure yesterday.

Stunning Madeleine Gurdon, 28, drew gasps of admiration after shedding more than a **STONE**.

Madeleine has worked furiously to lose weight because she thought she looked "flabby" in her engagement photographs last November.

She wore a body-hugging £7,500 dress for the church ceremony to bless the couple's marriage.

They formally wed at a register office a fortnight ago and planned to be at tiny St Botolph's Church in Burgh, Suffolk, last week.

But blizzards forced them to put off the ceremony — and the lavish private reception which

Before . . . "flabby" Maddy

So trim: Maddy and Andrew   **Picture: ARTHUR EDWARDS**

Continued on Page Three

● Just a cruel hoax
● Bombing goes on
● Iraq defeat looms

SADDAM Hussein was staring defeat in the face last night after his peace plan was exposed as a cruel hoax.

Allied chiefs believe his twisted offer to quit Kuwait proves his war effort is in its death throes.

Saddam's bid to trick the world was seen as a tactic to stall the inevitable destruction of his army.

But Allied warplanes have now been ordered to **CONTINUE** non-stop bombing against Iraqi

From TREVOR KAVANAGH in Riyadh and ALLAN HALL in New York

forces until they give up the fight.

And Allied commander General Norman Schwarzkopf has told U.S. President George Bush the war is now in its final days.

RETREAT

Bush branded the offer to leave Kuwait a "cruel hoax" after Saddam linked it to an impossible string of demands totally rejected by the West. Premier John

Major also denounced it as a "bogus sham".

But he added: "It is perhaps the first indication that Saddam now accepts himself he cannot win."

Hypocrite Saddam last night launched another Scud attack on Saudi Arabia — on the eastern oil port of Al Jubail.

Eye witnesses said a Scud was intercepted by Patriot missiles. No damage was reported.

Schwarzkopf believes demoralised Iraqis cannot withstand a huge Allied tank offensive

Continued on Page Four

THE Sun

THE PAPER THAT SUPPORTS OUR BOYS AND GIRLS

Monday, February 25, 1991   **25p**   Audited daily sale for January 3,742,454   Thought: You're doing us proud, lads

A SEA OF WHITE FLAGS

We've had enough! Soldiers of Iraq's crack Republican Guard surrender on the Saudi-Kuwait border yesterday

- **10,000 Iraqis give in**
- **100,000 troops on run**

TEN thousand Iraqi troops surrendered last night as Allied tanks stormed to the outskirts of Kuwait City.

They waved white flags in what U.S. Pentagon chiefs described as "the mother of all surrenders."

From TREVOR KAVANAGH at Allied Command HQ, Riyadh

One report said another 100,000 of Saddam's troops were fleeing the onslaught as tanks, headed by Britain's Desert Rats, roared into Iraq and Kuwait. And the Allies were "within hours" of retaking Kuwait

City in a desperate race to halt a massacre of innocent civilians.

Retreating Iraqis were said to be slaughtering children in a copy of Hitler's atrocities when he smelled defeat in 1945.

Desperate Saddam pleaded on Baghdad Radio with his troops in the desert: "Fight on, fight on, fight

Continued on Page Two

THE Sun

Tuesday, March 5, 1991 **25p** Audited daily sale for January 3,742,454 Thought: Corgis in the doghouse

Queen . . . "courageous"

QUEEN IS BITTEN IN CORGI FIGHT

Freed . . . hero pilot John Peters yesterday

ALL OUT!

By JOHN KAY

IRAQ said last night that **ALL** Western PoWs could be free by tonight.

The pledge, by its UN envoy, came as Tornado hero pilot John Peters and nine other Allied prisoners flew to safety after being freed in a "symbolic gesture."

Ambassador Abdul Amir al-Anbariy told TV reporters: "It's a matter of logistics.

"We are prepared to repatriate all so-called coalition

Continued on Page Five

Beaten . . John on Iraq TV

3 stitches after dogs turn nasty

By PHIL DAMPIER and JAMIE PYATT

THE Queen was bitten by one of her corgis as she tried to stop a savage fight between them, it was revealed last night.

She needed three stitches in her hand after the ten-strong pack turned nasty during a walk at Windsor Castle at the weekend.

The Queen Mother's

EXCLUSIVE

chauffeur John Collins was badly bitten and had to have a tetanus injection in hospital.

Staff rushed to help The Queen after the attack and took her back to the castle for treatment.

Top dog expert Roger Mugford said last night: "She was very lucky the injury was not worse.

"Corgis have powerful

Continued on Page Two

THE Sun

Wednesday, March 27, 1991 **25p** Audited daily sale for February 3,725,729 Thought: Hollywood and bust

£175 POLL TAX JOY FOR MILLIONS

By EBEN BLACK

POLL tax payers will face average bills this year of less than **£175**.

Environment Minister Michael Heseltine revealed the figure last night as the Government rushed through a move to chop £140 off every bill.

He said that eight million people — one in five of Britain's poll tax payers — will get extra help with paying.

They had faced cuts in rebates because their bills would have been too **LOW** to qualify.

In January, the Government announced £1.7billion in aid for those most hard hit by the poll tax.

Many of those who qualified under that scheme will still get **SOME** help.

But they will not get the full £100 rebate because reductions will be worked out after bills have been cut by £140.

Opposition parties had tried to block the Bill as it raced through Parliament.

But last night they backed down. Mr Heseltine warned councils to get the new bills

Continued on Page Two

MADONNA WITH THE BIG BOOBIES

Has she had op up top?

By GRAHAM DUDMAN and SHAN LANCASTER

ALLO ALLO! It's Madonna wiz ze beeg boobies — sparking claims that she has had breast IMPLANTS.

The superstar stunned fans by launching into a sexy strip on stage at Hollywood's Oscars ceremony — showing off a breath-taking new look.

Celebrities wolf-whistled and cheered as she peeled off a long white glove and tossed away her mink wrap.

GONE was her lean, muscular physique — the result of daily five-hour workouts. And **GONE** was the 34in bust which used to fit into bras shaped like ice cream cones. A photographer at Monday night's ceremony said: "She certainly looked a lot more full-figured than in the past."

Some fans claimed she was **PREGNANT**. Her spokeswoman Liz Rosenberg refused to comment.

PHOTOS

Fashion experts said 32-year-old Madonna's cleavage was the result of a push-up **BRA** worn under her shimmering skin-tight dress.

But last night, a Harley Street plastic surgeon examined photos taken at the ceremony and said: "She could well have had an implant."

Madonna stole the show at the 63rd awards in Los Angeles.

She did an impression of her movie idol Marilyn Monroe as she sang her Oscar-winning Sooner Or Later I Always Get My Man, from the film Dick Tracy.

Oscars special — Pages 8 and 9

So slim . . Madonna with 34in bust last year

Talk of the gown . . a full-figured Madonna wows fans during her performance at the ceremony

THE Sun

Thursday, March 28, 1991 **25p** Audited daily sale for February 3,725,729   Thought: Watch out bookies

Schwarzkopf . . . row over war

Stormin' Norman blasted by Bush

From ALLAN HALL in New York

GULF War hero Stormin' Norman Schwarzkopf came under fire last night — from President Bush and U.S. Defence Secretary Dick Cheney.

America's favourite soldier landed in hot water after complaining how he planned to wipe out Saddam Hussein's army but was ordered by the President to halt the ground offensive.

Mr Bush countered: "There was total agreement in terms of when this war should end."

Battle

And in a row that rocked Washington, Cheney added his own salvo.

He said the President's decision to halt military action was "coordinated with and concurred in by the commander in the field, General Schwarzkopf."

The remarks seemed to add up to a humbling of the outspoken, immensely popular General.

Schwarzkopf had said in a U.S. television interview with David Frost that he had recommended that Allied forces should "continue the march" against fleeing Iraqi forces.

The Allied military

Continued on Page Nine

SHERGAR 'IS ALIVE'

Wonder horse . . . Walter Swinburn on Shergar in 1981, his Derby-winning year

He's in Channel Isles but we want money, gang tells insurers

By JOHN KAY

KIDNAPPED wonder horse Shergar is ALIVE, shocked insurance chiefs were told yesterday.

The sensational claim was made by a group of bounty hunters seeking a reward for finding the £10million Derby winner.

Nothing had been heard of Shergar since he was snatched from owner the Aga Khan's Irish Stud in 1983.

HOPE

The kidnappers, believed to be an IRA gang, were thought to have **SHOT** him within 48 hours of disappearing.

But stunned underwriters, who

EXCLUSIVE

paid out £3,625,000 to Shergar's owners, were told he is now happily grazing in a field "somewhere in the Channel Islands."

Steve Chappell, deputy chairman of Lloyds Bloodstock Committee, confirmed a middle-man had tried to negotiate a £365,000 "finders' fee."

He said: "We have been informed Shergar is alive. But we have no concrete proof and I am very sceptical.

"It would seem someone is trying to negotiate a payment, but I have made it clear that Lloyds will never pay a finders' fee or ransom for the return of any stolen horse."

Shergar won the Derby by a

Continued on Page Two

Wednesday, April 24, 1991   **25p**   Audited daily sale for March 3,745,958   Thought: Cheap remark

Perfick! Major's new tax helps the little guy

By TREVOR KAVANAGH
Political Editor

PREMIER John Major last night freed millions of ordinary folk from crippling Poll Tax bills.

His new Council Tax, based on property values, scraps the hated system which meant a duke and a dustman paid the same.

Under the scheme, the more your home is worth, the more you will pay.

Hard-up young nurses, students and apprentices will pay **NOTHING** because of rebates they will get.

The simple tax, unveiled by Environment Secretary Michael Heseltine, will slash hundreds of millions of pounds off the cost of collection.

Each home — including council properties — will get **ONE** bill based on its value, to be worked out by a local assessor.

Election

Homes will be placed within seven price bands, ranging from £40,000 to £160,000 and over.

The charge is calculated on an average of two adults per home — and people living alone will get 25 per cent off.

Typical bills will range from £287 to £688 for the most pricey home.

Two out of three people will pay **LESS** than under the Poll Tax.

One in three families will pay under £300 and only one in seven bills will be over £500.

Tory chairman Chris Patten said the Party is now "under starter's orders" for a triumphant general election. He

Continued on Page Two

BUMPER SHOW

A dance group featuring seven **PREGNANT** women will put on a show about motherhood in Bow, East London, on Friday.

ROTNERS

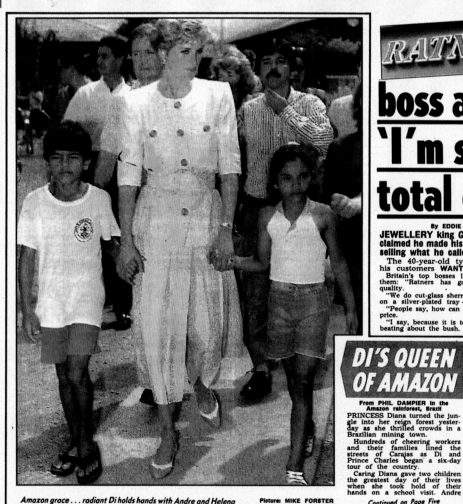

Amazon grace . . . radiant Di holds hands with Andre and Helena   **Picture: MIKE FORSTER**

boss admits: 'I'm selling total crap'

By EDDIE FITZMAURICE

JEWELLERY king Gerald Ratner yesterday claimed he made his £335million fortune by selling what he called "TOTAL CRAP."

The 40-year-old tycoon said that is what his customers **WANT.**

Britain's top bosses listened amazed as he told them: "Ratners has got very little to do with quality.

"We do cut-glass sherry decanters with six glasses on a silver-plated tray — and it only costs £4.95.

"People say, how can you sell this for such a low price.

"I say, because it is total crap. There is no point beating about the bush. We even sell a pair of gold earrings for under £1, which is cheaper than a prawn sandwich from Marks & Spencer.

"But I have to say the sandwich will probably last longer than the earrings."

TASTE

Mr Ratner, who has 2,000 stores worldwide, made his astonishing admission in a speech to the Institute of Directors at London's Albert Hall.

He told them: "Ratner shops will never win awards for design. They are not in the best possible taste. Some people say they can't even see the jewellery for all the posters and banners in the window.

"But it's interesting

Continued on Page Four

DI'S QUEEN OF AMAZON

From PHIL DAMPIER in the Amazon rainforest, Brazil

PRINCESS Diana turned the jungle into her reign forest yesterday as she thrilled crowds in a Brazilian mining town.

Hundreds of cheering workers and their families lined the streets of Carajas as Di and Prince Charles began a six-day tour of the country.

Caring Diana gave two children the greatest day of their lives when she took hold of their hands on a school visit. Andre

Continued on Page Five

THE Sun

Friday, May 24, 1991   **25p**   Audited daily sale for April 3,688,645   Thought: Lame excuse

ALL MY FAULT!

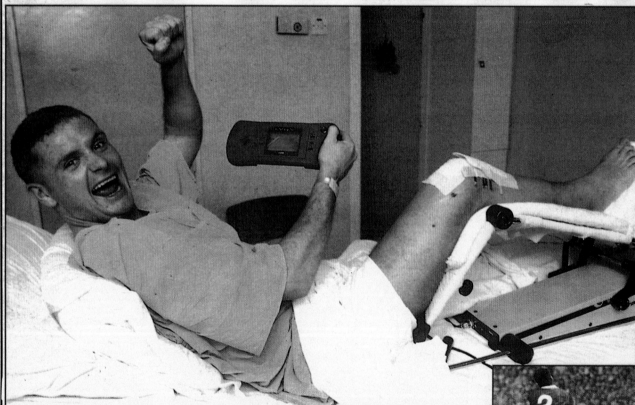

Fighting to get fit yesterday . . . Gazza shows soccer fans he won't let his knee injury get him down   Picture by MARTIN CULLUM

Gazza opens his heart to The Sun

By JOHN RICHARDSON

GAZZA sat up in his hospital bed yesterday and told The Sun: "It's all my own fault."

In an exclusive interview, the 23-year-old soccer superstar said he couldn't believe how daft he was to make the tackle which caused his shattering knee injury.

He said: "God alone knows what went through my mind, because I don't." The Spurs star, who was carried off in agony after 15 minutes of Saturday's FA Cup Final, wept when his team mates burst into his hospital room after the match with the Cup and his medal.

In the interview Gazza reveals his devastation as the biggest day of his life turned to disaster — but bounces back to warn critics: "Don't write me off, I'll be back stronger than ever."

Crunch . . . the moment of agony

READ HIS STORY: Pages 4 & 5

THE Sun

Wednesday, May 29, 1991   **25p**   Audited daily sale for April 3,688,645   Thought: They deserve it

ROLLS BOSS TAKES A 10% PAY CUT

By MARK SOLOMONS

ROLLS-ROYCE boss Lord Tombs has taken a 10 per cent pay cut to help save the troubled engine makers, he revealed yesterday.

But angry workers still threatened an all-out strike over plans to sack 6,000.

Last year, the chairman got a huge 51 per cent increase in wages and bonuses. Yesterday he told a stormy AGM his yearly pay had fallen from £150,000 to £135,000.

And he will not get a bonus this year.

It is a third of what other industry chiefs earn, added the 67-year-old peer. But a cut "is appropriate." Pay has been frozen for directors. Managers will only get a five per cent rise.

But union boss Fred Hodgson — among hundreds of demonstrators outside the London meeting — said: "The workforce feel bitter. There used to be a *Continued on Page Eight*

SUN WINS GULF CASH VICTORY FOR OUR BOYS

By JOHN KAY

THE SUN'S battle to win a fair deal for the families of Our Boys killed in the Gulf War ended in victory last night.

Defence Secretary Tom King pledged that every penny of the £3million raised for the fund will go to relatives of the 42 dead.

Mr King was stung into action after Sun readers demanded that the Government hand over the cash.

Last night Liberal Democrat MP Sir Cyril Smith, who alerted the The Sun to the scandal, said: "I am delighted and I offer my congratulations and thanks to you."

JUSTICE

The mother of 17-year-old Fusilier Conrad Cole, the youngest British soldier to die in the Gulf, said: "I wanted to see justice done.

"It's bad enough trying to come to terms with a death, without having to find yourself fighting for what you should be entitled to."

Mrs Susan Cole said she had been forced to "beg" for cash from the Gulf Trust.

NICE WON MY SUN
Pages 4 & 5

The Sun's battling Page One on Monday

Hero Conrad Cole, youngest Gulf victim

Sun SPORT

Wednesday, May 29, 1991 ★★★★

Lamb tells England: Stuff you!

By JOHN ETHERIDGE

ALLAN LAMB last night insisted he never wants to captain England again.

Lamb skippered England in three Test matches and has been Graham Gooch's vice-captain for the past 18 months — but now he has quit as understudy.

It is Lamb's angry response to being told by Gooch that he no longer wants him as his No.2.

Lamb, 36, said: "In view of the uncertainty and speculation that has been prevalent in the last few days, I wish to clarify my position relating to the vice-captaincy of the England team.

"During the recent Texaco Trophy series, I've had long discussions with Graham Gooch. He has explained his personal feelings and why he and the England committee did not want me to remain as official vice-captain.

Future

"However, I feel it would be beneficial, both personally and for the team if, in future, I was not considered for leadership of the England team on the field during
● Turn to Page 36

LAMB... quit as No.2

©News Group Newspapers Ltd. Published and printed by News Group Newspapers Ltd, 1 Virginia St, London E1 9BD; 071-782-4000. Registered as a newspaper at the PO No. 8,706. Austria 21sch, Channel Islands 26p, France 7fr, Germany 2.80dm, Greece 200dr, Italy 1700li, Portugal 180esc, Spain 180pts, Malta 25c.

22

9 770307 268038

£8,000 A WEEK BAIT FOR CHRIS

By BRIAN WOOLNOUGH

CHRIS WADDLE'S wages will rocket to £8,000 a week if Marseille win the European Cup tonight.

Victory over Red Star Belgrade will see Waddle double his pay and pick up a £100,000 bonus to go with the £1million he has already earned playing in France.

Every man in Marseille's 20-strong first team squad will collect £100,000 for victory. Multi-millionaire president Bernard Tapie will ask Waddle to stay in France for the rest of his career at the new, sky-high wages.

Tapie will stop at nothing to make
● Turn to Page 38

DAVID PLATT . . . Marseille are moving in

FROGS WANT PLATT TO JOIN WADDLE

SUN SOCCER EXCLUSIVE

EUROPEAN Cup finalists Marseille have begun moves to buy David Platt and link him in a £10m English strike-force with Chris Waddle.

I can reveal that the mega-rich French club have already been in

From ALEX MONTGOMERY in Sydney

touch with English agents to establish if Platt would fancy the move.

As they prepared for the biggest game in their history — tonight's European Cup Final against Red Star Belgrade in Bari — Marseille were already building for next season. They talked to agents in England making it clear they wanted Platt, whether they win the European Cup or not.

Villa, who had already accepted a £4.5m bid from Italian club Bari, will do business, despite parting company with boss Jo Venglos last night.

And Platt, who turned down Bari because such a deal "wasn't right for me," will be tempted.

He arrived in Australia with the England tour party last night to hear the news that Venglos had left Villa Park — now he has to decide his own future.

Marseille owner Bernard Tapie has used his millions to transform the club into one of Europe's top teams. And the fact that Waddle has been such a sensational success in France since his £4.5m move has convinced Tapie to go for Platt.

Compete

The super-wealthy businessman — he recently bought sports wear company Adidas — is determined that Marseille will continue to compete for the world's best players.

Platt's emergence as
● Turn to Page 39

HAGAR THE HORRIBLE   By CHRIS BROWNE

MYSTIKO IN RACE FEAR

MYSTIKO has only a 50-50 chance of running in tomorrow's Derby.

The 2,000 Guineas hero is being treated for a corn problem, trainer Clive Brittain revealed yesterday.

Mystiko, now 100-30 with a run, faces a dawn fitness test today.

French challenger Toulon is the new Derby favourite at 5-2.

● Full story — Pages 26, 27.

Put your offers in now for Wright, Saunders

England's tour men flop: P30

By JOHN RICHARDSON

DERBY have set a Monday deadline for clubs to buy Mark Wright and Dean Saunders.

And that will spark the biggest transfer scramble for years.

Leeds have already made a £3million bid for Saunders, while Liverpool are favourites for England defender Wright.

But a host of other clubs — both at home and abroad — are sure to join the chase.

Relegated Derby delivered their "Come and get them" message yesterday.

Chairman Robert Maxwell ordered manager Arthur Cox to contact clubs who have already made offers for one — or both — players.

And Maxwell insisted any bids should be made in writing by 5pm next Monday.

Leeds boss Wilkinson

● Turn to Page 30

FROGS WANT KENNY AT £1M A YEAR

DALGLISH . . . locked in meeting

He has secret talks with Marseille boss

By JIM BLACK

KENNY DALGLISH was locked in secret talks for 12 hours at the weekend as Marseille try to make him their new boss.

The French club's mega-rich president Bernard Tapie has offered Dalglish £1million-a-year to tempt him back into football.

EXCLUSIVE

Dalglish walked out as Liverpool boss five months ago, claiming he could not stand the pressure — and has NEVER been back to Anfield.

Signal

Liverpool have an agreement with Dalglish which stops him joining another British club without their permission — but there is nothing to stop him going abroad.

And now Marseille — Chris Waddle's club — are ready to pounce, elbowing aside Frog rivals Monaco's bid to land Dalglish.

Tapie revealed last night he would announce a big-name signing after Marseille's French Cup Final against Monaco on Saturday. And he admitted: "You're going to be surprised."

Dalglish's arrival would signal the departure of Franz Beckenbauer. He

● Turn to Page 31

HAGAR THE HORRIBLE   By CHRIS BROWNE

EAT! DRINK! AND BORROW! IN OUR LINE OF WORK WE MAY DIE TOMORROW!

RIGHT!

INCIDENTALLY, I'M NOT COMING TO WORK TOMORROW

THE Sun

Tuesday, June 18, 1991   **25p**   Audited daily sale for May 3,627,611   Thought: The gloves are off

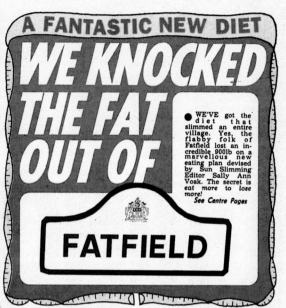
Back op threat to pain racked Charles

PRINCE Charles is suffering from a crumbling disc in his back and is in "intense pain," it was revealed last night.

He has cancelled his engagements for two weeks and been told he faces an operation unless he rests.

Surgeon John Webb, who operated on the Prince after his polo fall last year, said: "He has a severe problem. He must rest.

"If he ignores it, he may need surgery."

One of the top events Charles has pulled out of this week is Royal Ascot, which starts today.

Advice

Mr Webb told the Prince last week that he needed complete rest.

He agreed to give up playing polo, but went ahead with engagements in London, Yorkshire and Scotland.

The Prince also rode in the Queen's Birthday Parade on Saturday.

Afterwards he telephoned Mr Webb, who repeated his earlier advice.

The Prince then accepted that the surgeon had been right in the first place and that only

Continued on Page Five

MAGGIE SAVAGES JACQUES THE RIPPER

Nov 1990 . . what The Sun told Delors

From **SIMON WALTERS** in Chicago

MARGARET Thatcher last night launched a devastating attack on EC president Jacques Delors' plan for a United States of Europe.

She branded the proposal a disastrous attempt to crush Britain's national identity that was "doomed to failure."

The ex-Premier said a giant Euro superstate would also:

● Wreck NATO and possibly become an enemy of the USA

● Set up a "wealth wall" to replace the Berlin Wall and stop Eastern Europe becoming more westernised.

SCORN

Mrs Thatcher said she was "in full agreement" with Premier John Major's firm opposition to a federal Europe.

But her explosive remarks are bound to fuel the split between Tory pro and anti-marketeers.

Mrs Thatcher departed from her prepared speech to fire a withering blast at Mr Delors.

She criticised his attempt just hours earlier to steamroller the 12 EC nations into joint economic, defence and foreign policies.

She said: "A new document with sweeping powers has emerged in Brussels.

"Our Foreign Secretary opposed the whole-

Continued on Page Two

THE Sun

Monday, June 24, 1991   25p   Audited daily sale for May 3,627,611   Thought: Taking the Michael

MACHETE MAN GIVES HIMSELF UP TO The Sun

By NEIL SYSON

A MAN wanted for questioning after a machete attack in which his girlfriend's hand was chopped off has turned himself in — thanks to The Sun.

We persuaded jobless Chris Woolnough to give himself up after he rang us to give an interview. He had been hunted since an armed police siege on his bedsit.

Just before walking into a police station at Gillingham, Kent, last night, he insisted: "I'm not a violent man." Woolnough had been dating victim Sylvia Eastwood, 23, for eight months after meeting her at a disco.

They split last week after a row but Woolnough went to her home in Chatham at 1am last Thursday to try to patch things up.

Sylvia's hand was

Continued on Page Two

PRINCESS MICHAEL SOLD ROYAL FAMILY SILVER

EXCLUSIVE

By MIKE RIDLEY

PRINCESS Michael of Kent sold her husband's family silver to pay bank debts.

But long-suffering Prince Michael never knew what his wife was up to and was duped about where the cash came from, it is revealed today.

The astonishing truth is told by the couple's former private secretary, John Barratt, an unwitting accomplice in the Princess's scheme to sell her Royal husband's heirlooms.

Barratt, 57, has written a devastating book about his years of Royal service — and starting today, an exclusive Sun serialisation reveals the secrets even 50-year-old Prince Michael did not know.

Princess Michael, 46, ordered Barratt to fly two travel bags crammed with valuables out of the country to Switzerland.

There he handed them over to a mystery man at a clandestine airport rendezvous, before having a cup of coffee and catching the next plane back to London.

SHOCKING

Barratt says: "I now cannot believe I actually went through with it.

"In almost 20 years' service with the Royal Family, and being privy to many secrets, it is the most shocking thing I was ever asked to do."

Barratt also reveals how he battled to keep the bankers at bay after Princess Michael sent accounts into the red.

He finally quit in disgust at her bullying.

Barratt is the highest-ranking aide ever to speak out in public about private Palace life.

He was Lord Mountbatten's private secretary and a confidant of Prince Charles.

Secret flight to Switzerland: Centre Pages

Princess Michael . . . her lavish lifestyle put her in the red

THE Sun

Tuesday, June 25, 1991   **25p**   Audited daily sale for May 3,627,611   Thought: Court-ing couple

OTHER MEN IN PRINCESS PUSHY'S LIFE
SEE CENTRE PAGES

NEW BALLS PLEASE

Lynda . . chats on phone

Relf . . . wrote love poems

Wimbledon line judge Lynda runs off with top umpire

EXCLUSIVE

By JOHN ASKILL

A TOP Wimbledon umpire has run off with a senior woman line judge.

He is John Relf, 52, full-time administrator of the British Tennis Umpires' Association.

She is Welsh divorcee Lynda Varlek, 42.

They should have been on court at Wimbledon yesterday, but rain washed out play.

This is the ball-by-ball end of Relf's love match with his wife Helen, 55:

15-love: She stumbles on poems written by her husband to her rival and photos of Mrs Varlek at their home.

ROMANCE

30-love: She accuses him of a love affair and kicks him out of their home. He returns after six weeks, promising to give up his romance.

40-love: She catches him chatting to Lynda on the phone in his office. She grabs the phone and tells her: "Stay away from my husband."

Game, set and match: John walks out of their

Continued on Page Three

£30m BILL AFTER GULF WAR SLIP

By NEIL SYSON

DEFENCE chiefs are spending £30 million replacing thousands of lap-top computers like the one packed with Gulf War secrets that was stolen from a car.

The Zenith Super Sport is considered a security risk because the disc which stores information cannot be removed.

The news broke yesterday as Wing Commander David Farquhar faced a court martial, accused of allowing battle plans to be stolen from his parked staff car. Three briefcases

Continued on Page Seven

Howay from it all . . . Gazza soaks up the Algarve sun as he recovers from his operation   Picture: MARTIN CULLUM

- **SUN** guys have all the luck! While we rain-lashed Brits suffered at home, crocked soccer ace Gazza was baking with an orange juice in 90° heat on the Algarve.
- The Spurs and England ace, recovering from his Cup Final knee operation, flew back to Britain yesterday

PICTURE EXCLUSIVE

for transfer talks saying: "I feel great, I'm on the mend.
- He was one of the few not feeling the Monday blues as rain wiped out the first day of Wimbledon, and forced the Test Match to be abandoned

Gazza is ours — Back Page

Gazza takes it kneesy by pool

THE Sun

Wednesday, July 31, 1991 **25p** Audited daily sale for June 3,634,820 Thought: Nessun stormer

PAVAWETTI

Wet a difference a Di makes! Bedraggled Princess Diana is spiky-haired from watching opera star Pavarotti with Prince Charles last night in a thrilling Hyde Park show seen live on BSkyB. The Royal pair sheltered under plastic sheets as pouring rain hit the free concert for 125,000 fans

JUST ONE MORE WETTO: FULL STORY–Pages 4 and 5

THE Sun

Thursday, September 5, 1991   **25p**   Estimated average daily sale, August 3,745,474   TV: Pages 28 and 29

ZINGO

MAJOR IN NOVEMBER POLL ALERT

BRITAIN will go to the polls in November if the Tories continue to keep a strong lead over Labour.

The move was signalled yesterday after Premier John Major ordered another cut in interest rates — from 11 to 10.5 per cent.

The Prime Minister is keeping his troops on general election standby, despite warnings from Ministers to wait until spring.

Polling day could be November 7, although later in the month is more likely.

Mr Major is ready to order further interest cuts soon if inflation drops sharply to the four per cent expected for August and September.

Full story — Page 2

VAT MAN IN QUIZ OVER VICE MURDER

By NEIL SYSON and MARY COMERFORD

A VAT inspector was being questioned by police last night over the murder of vice girl Sharon Hoare and attacks on two other prostitutes.

Detectives arrested him at a flat near Sharon's and took away a video of the film Pretty Woman.

The 24-year-old man is being quizzed about the attempted murder of hooker Lucy Christopher, and an attack on a third girl on Monday evening.

Sharon, 19, was found strangled and beaten at her home in Brompton Park, West London, on August 10.

Lucy, 24, was attacked at her flat in South

Continued on Page Two

DES FALLS FOR HIS GONG BANGER

She's 30 years his junior

BONG! Actress Jodie takes her pick and it's Des

By STUART HIGGINS

DES O'CONNOR has fallen for the sexy girl who bangs his gong in his new TV series Take Your Pick — and she is 30 years his junior.

Dashing Des, 59, is seeing 29-year-old actress and singer Jodie Wilson. The blonde Aussie is the same age as Des's last wife — and his oldest daughter Karen.

The couple met at Christmas when Jodie played Cinderella and Des was Buttons in panto at Plymouth.

Des announced the collapse of his four-year marriage to Swiss beauty Jay Rufer last March.

Then Des and Jodie were reunited when she turned up to audition as a hostess for a new version of Take Your Pick.

Sun EXCLUSIVE

A Thames TV insider said: "Their eyes literally met again across the gong and that was it — bells were ringing from that moment on."

Last night a spokesman for Des said: "Des and Jodie are seeing each other regularly.

"They met after the marriage had foundered and Des had left the marital home.

"At the moment they are enjoying each other's company. As for the future, we will have to wait and see."

In Take Your Pick, which will be seen next year, Jodie bangs the

Continued on Page 9

BONG! Des is in love.

THE Sun

Friday, October 4, 1991   25p   Audited daily sale for August 3,747,234   Today's TV: Pages 28 and 29

I'M THE TART

I cost DPP his job, says Samantha of King's Cross

Vice girl . . . Samantha and her boyfriend last night   Picture: MARTIN CULLUM

EXCLUSIVE

By NEIL SYSON, ROBERT KELLAWAY and GRAHAM DUDMAN

THIS is the 23-year-old vice girl who cost law chief Sir Allan Green his job.

Brunette Samantha works the seedy streets of King's Cross in London where she charges £25 for full sex.

Sir Allan, 56, resigned as Director of Public Prosecutions yesterday after police booked him talking to Samantha from his car.

When asked how she felt last night, Samantha yelled: "How the **** do you think I feel? I lost the ******* Director of Public Prosecutions his job!"

Samantha, who lives with her boyfriend in a run-down tower block, said at first: "I'm not interested in talking to you, no matter how much money you offer. Money isn't everything."

But then she asked: "How much would you be talking about?" The Sun had offered no money.

Sir Allan, an £82,775-a-year barrister, is married with two children. He had been spotted before by

Continued on Page Two

Sir Allan Green . . he quit

SEX SCANDAL OF DISGRACED LAW CHIEF: Pages 2,3,4,5,6

THE Sun

Maxwell mystery

Wednesday, November 6, 1991 **25p** Audited daily sale for September 3,762,151 **Today's TV: Pages 28 and 29**

DID HE FALL...

Cap'n Bob .. Robert Maxwell on the deck of his £12million yacht. He had been cruising off the Canaries

DID HE JUMP?

By SIMON HUGHES and IAN HEPBURN

TYCOON Robert Maxwell was found dead in the Atlantic last night — 14 hours after mysteriously going missing from his yacht.

The naked body of the 68-year-old Daily Mirror boss was hauled from the sea by a helicopter.

Investigators were asking three questions about the death of Maxwell, who had been cruising off the Canaries on board the £12million Lady Ghislaine. Did he acciden-

Tycoon found dead in sea

tally fall? Did he jump to his death to escape increasing pressures from his debt-laden businesses?

Or did an Arab assassin sneak aboard — seeking revenge over recent claims that Maxwell was linked to the Israeli secret service Mossad?

ACCIDENT? The media magnate may

have plunged over the 3ft rails surrounding the deck of his 450-ton yacht after he emerged from his cabin at 4.45am.

Maxwell was a light sleeper who often took the air in the early hours while at sea.

He was often clad only in a bath towel — which would have been washed away in the waves. Spanish servicemen who found Max-

well said there were no signs of violence on the body.

SUICIDE? Personal and business burdens had mounted on 20-stone Maxwell in recent weeks. Debt of the huge complex of Maxwell firms is much greater than accounts of his public companies show, it is revealed in a Financial Times investigation today.

The total debt could have been about £3.3 billion early this year. By floating Mirror Group shares and disposing of other assets that total was reduced to £2.2 billion. But

Continued on Page Three

FULL STORY – Pages 2, 3, 4, 5, 6, 7, 8, 14 and 27

THE Sun

Monday, November 25, 1991 **25p** Audited daily sale for October 3,705,400 **Today's TV: Pages 16 and 17**

FREDDIE IS DEAD

Showman . . . Freddie draped in a Union Flag during a typically flamboyant performance

1946

1991

ROCK star Freddie Mercury is dead — just two days after he confirmed he had AIDS.

The Queen singer's parents were at his bedside as he slipped away late last night at his £1million London mansion.

His spokesman Roxy Meade

By STEPHANIE SCAWEN

said just before midnight: "Freddie Mercury died peacefully this evening. It was the result of bronchial-pneumonia, brought on by AIDS."

The 45-year-old gay star's death stunned the showbiz world. Comedian Kenny Everett, a close friend, said: "He

burned the candle at both ends and in the middle."

Radio One DJ Simon Bates said: "I can't believe that he's gone so suddenly.

"Freddie was a man who played hard and paid the most dreadful price. The saddest thing is that the world of entertainment has lost a great genius." Simon was working

GARTER LOAD OF THESE BRIDES
-CENTRE PAGES

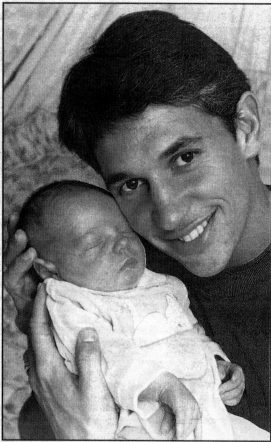

Royal comfort . . . Fergie has supported Gary as son George fights leukaemia

FERGIE SENDS CARD TO GARY

EXCLUSIVE by STUART HIGGINS

FERGIE has sent a personal message of hope to soccer star Gary Lineker and his wife as they keep a vigil at the bedside of their nine-week-old son, George.

Her handwritten letter went to London's Great Ormond St hospital where George is said to be "improving slowly" after chemotherapy treatment for leukaemia.

The Duchess of York is one of thousands of well-wishers from all over the world who have sent cards and letters to the England soccer captain and his wife Michelle.

Mum-of-two Fergie is president of the children's charity Action Research and patron of the Sick Children's Trust.

Yesterday, overwhelmed Gary said: "If good wishes meant anything to our little George he would have recovered in an hour."

Despite his troubles, Gary has given the go-ahead for a light hearted ad featuring him smiling.

The advert for football cards, filmed before George's tragic illness, shows Gary grinning as children swap cards.

TV CHIEFS GRILL RUSTIE

CHEF Rustie Lee was grilled for two hours by TV-am bosses yesterday over The Sun's revelations that she was paid to plug food products on her show.

The station's lawyers quizzed her after we told how firms used her for product placement — strictly banned by TV rules.

She then sped away from the company's London HQ without

Continued on Page Seven

Mirror Mirror on the wall, who is the biggest crook of all?

Maxwell . . . "swindler"

ROBERT Maxwell was branded the "crook of the century" last night by angry Daily Mirror pensioners.

They hit out as the Serious Fraud Office revealed it is to probe the scandal of the Mirror pension fund's missing millions.

The SFO, which exposed the Guinness share-rigging scandal, was already investigating a loan to Maxwell. Experts fear up to £300million may have been switched from the fund to Mr Maxwell's private companies before his mystery death last month.

By JOHN KAY and NICK PARKER

WORRIED

Former Sporting Life editor Ossie Fletcher, 70, said: "The indications are that Maxwell will go down as the crook of the century."

Ossie paid in contributions for 26 years to give him a pension of £20,000 a year.

He said: "I began to get seriously worried about the pension fund some months ago, but never dreamed it would be as bad as this."

New Mirror Group chairman Ernie Burrington said Maxwell's misappropriation of pension cash was "the increasingly desperate acts of an increasingly desperate man."

And last night, it *Continued on Page Two*

THE Sun

Tuesday, December 10, 1991   **25p**   Audited daily sale for October 3,705,400   Today's TV: Pages 24 and 25

Infant school teacher is world's top groupie

-SEE CENTRE PAGES

Health fear for Strike It Lucky Michael

■ EXCLUSIVE

By ANDY COULSON and CHRIS HUGHES

SHOWBIZ stars are growing concerned for the health of Strike It Lucky host Michael Barrymore.

The 38-year-old funnyman has lost weight and is suffering from spells of tiredness, according to his agent.

The news comes as Michael is filming a new series of the quiz show for LWT.

Originally to be screened as hour-long specials, the shows have been cut down to 45 minutes.

It is thought the decision was made to ease pressure on Michael. Producer Ian Hamilton was "unhappy" with some of the show's material.

Manic

One celebrity, who asked not to be named, said: "Michael is usually such a healthy and energetic bloke. It's terrible to see him like this."

Michael's agent Ann Chudleigh blames the weight loss on his grief over the death of his father-in-law more than a year ago.

Eddie Cocklin, dad of Michael's wife Cheryl, helped him rise from a seaside comic to a millionaire entertainer.

Michael is now one of telly's top stars, famous for his catchphrase "Awight?" and manic, long-strided runs.

Strike It Lucky
Continued on Page Seven

Shattered . . . Michael and wife Cheryl, whose dad helped him to fame

'F' OFF

Major wins fight on 'federal' but £ is ambushed

PREMIER John Major scored a major triumph at the Euro summit last night by getting the "F-word" dropped.

He won agreement that the word "Federalism" in the new EC treaty will be replaced by a reference to "ever closer union" of European peoples.

But he was ambushed by heavyweight EC states who ganged up and ordered Britain to scrap the pound by 1999.

The decisions came after a day of intense and sometimes fraught negotiations at Maastricht.

FINAL

Mr Major had warned all along that a treaty containing the word "federal" could not be endorsed by the British government.

Dutch foreign minister Hans van den Broek warned that Britain would be expected to give ground in return at today's final summit session.

"That will be the time

By TREVOR KAVANAGH and EBEN BLACK

for paying, or receiving certain benefits or bonuses," he said.

Mr Major was outnumbered 11-1 by Common Market leaders who want to lock us into a rigid timetable for a single European currency.

Mr Major's demand for Westminster MPs to have the last say was swept aside.

The 11, led by the Italians and Dutch, agreed the final countdown to a single currency should start by

Continued on Page Two

MAXWELL SONS HIT BY FREEZE

THE son of disgraced Mirror Group publisher Robert Maxwell had his worldwide personal fortune of £450m frozen by the High Court yesterday.

Kevin Maxwell, 32, was also ordered to surrender his passport along with brother Ian, 35.

Row

Kevin has put up for sale his £1.7m mansion home in London's Chelsea.

Full story — Page Two

THE Sun

Thursday, February 6, 1992   **25p**   Estimated daily sale for January 3,661,350   Today's TV: Pages 36 and 37

IT'S PADDY PANTSDOWN

Still close . . . Paddy Ashdown gets the support of his loyal wife Jane yesterday   Picture by ARTHUR EDWARDS

HE SAYS:
I had 5-month fling
with my secretary

WIFE SAYS:
We've been happy
for thirty years

IT was the day Liberal Democrat leader Paddy Ashdown had owned up to a five-month love affair with his ex-secretary — but he cuddled wife Jane and vowed it would not wreck their marriage.

Jane clung to her 50-year-old husband on the steps of their London home and declared: "We have been perfectly happy together for 30 years."

When asked about the next 30 years, Mr Ashdown said: "It'll last more than that." Jane, 51, laughed as she added: "I'll be lucky — I will be very old by then."

The couple joked just three hours after Mr Ashdown admitted he had been caught with his pants down over a fling in 1986

By PASCOE WATSON

with Tricia Howard, who was then his secretary.

He told a news conference at Westminster: "This has been an extremely painful experience but it is one which all involved, and especially Jane, my family and

Continued on Page Three

THE ASHDOWN AFFAIR: Pages 2,3,4,5,6,7,8,9

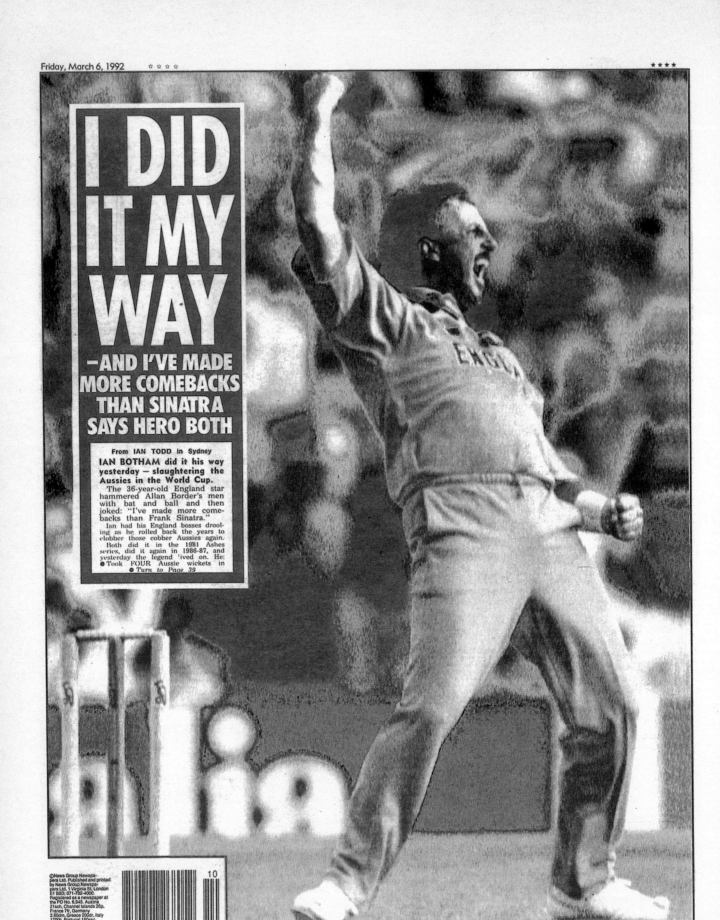

I DID IT MY WAY

—AND I'VE MADE MORE COMEBACKS THAN SINATRA SAYS HERO BOTH

From IAN TODD in Sydney

IAN BOTHAM did it his way yesterday — slaughtering the Aussies in the World Cup.

The 36-year-old England star hammered Allan Border's men with bat and ball and then joked: "I've made more comebacks than Frank Sinatra."

Ian had his England bosses drooling as he rolled back the years to clobber those cobber Aussies again.

Both did it in the 1981 Ashes series, did it again in 1986-87, and yesterday the legend 'lived on. He:

● Took FOUR Aussie wickets in
● *Turn to Page 39*

10

9 770307 268052

THE SUN

Thursday, April 9, 1992   25p   Today's TV: Pages 40 and 41   Audited daily sale for February 3,651,641

PHOTO FINISH

By TREVOR KAVANAGH
Political Editor

TORY hopes rose last night as opinion polls showed they were heading for a photo finish with Labour.

A Gallup poll for today's Daily Telegraph puts the Tories on 38.5 per cent, Labour 38 and the Liberal Democrats 20.

John Major's team

also had a 0.5 lead in the same survey last week.

Labour are on 39 in a Mori poll for The Times — just one point ahead of the Tories after having a seven-point lead last week.

An ICM poll for The Guardian shows Labour and Tories both on 38 points with the Lib-Dems on 20.

The same poll last week showed Labour four points ahead.

The polls confirm that millions of voters have waited until the last minute before making up their minds. Tory leaders believe they have won back wavering supporters who were

Continued on Page Two

Arthur Ashe . . . operation

TENNIS CHAMP ASHE HAS AIDS

From ALLAN HALL
in New York

TENNIS legend Arthur Ashe has AIDS, it was revealed last night.

The former Wimbledon champ contracted the killer virus from blood he was given during a heart operation 12 years ago.

Ashe, 48, underwent quadruple bypass surgery before screening was introduced to avoid AIDS infection through transfusions.

Star

AIDS was diagnosed late last year and Ashe has been taking the drug AZT in an attempt to hold the virus at bay.

The star — first black man to win a Grand Slam tournament — is one of nearly 5,000 people in America under death sentence through tainted blood.

Ashe, married with a five-year-old daughter, reached the pinnacle of his career in 1975 when he beat Jimmy Connors to take the men's singles title at Wimbledon.

The fitness fanatic seemed to be in his physical prime before a heart attack struck him in 1979.

He was just 36 and ranked No 7 in the world.

Ashe, son of a Virginia policeman, had his op later that year.

It left a ten-inch scar

Continued on Page 13

If Kinnock wins today will the last person to leave Britain please turn out the lights

ELECTION DAY SPECIAL

IT'S D-day folks — the day you make the big decision about who you want to run our great country.

You know our views on the subject but we don't want to influence you in your final judgment on

who will be Prime Minister.

But if it's a bald bloke with wispy red hair and two K's in his surname, we'll see you at the airport!

Goodnight and thank you for everything.

STATE OF THE PARTIES

TORIES	**324**	
LABOUR	**266**	
LIB-DEM	**16**	

MAJOR BACK AT No 10

By TREVOR KAVANAGH and SIMON WALTERS

CHAMPAGNE corks popped in Tory headquarters early today as jubilant John Major stormed to victory in a sensational election upset.

He wiped the smile off Welsh windbag Neil Kinnock's face by taking his party to a record fourth term in power.

The Premier headed back to Downing Street with a comfortable, overall, working majority of at least 15 seats.

And after boosting his own majority in Huntingdon by a whopping 9,000 votes, he quietly described the Tory triumph as "a satisfactory result, the right Government."

He said: "We can push on with recovery for Britain, which we all wish to see."

Distraught Mr Kinnock saw his dreams of power shattered as he watched the results on a hotel TV in his Welsh constituency.

It was a devastating blow for a man who staked his political life on a Socialist landslide — and convinced himself he was going to win.

Instead, his hopes were crushed by voters

Continued on Page Two

POLL SPECIAL—Pages 2, 3, 4, 5, 6, 7, 9, 10, 11, 17, 19

THE Sun

Friday, April 24, 1992   25p   Today's TV: Pages 28 and 29   Audited daily sale for March 3,629,449

SECRET OF LIFE THE UNIVERSE AND EVERYTHING

SEE PAGE SIX

Target ... Mr Ashdown

Boy of 9 uncovers IRA plot to murder Ashdown

EXCLUSIVE

By IAN HEPBURN and ROSS KANIUK

AN IRA plot to assassinate Liberal Democrat leader Paddy Ashdown has been exposed by a boy of nine.

The youngster stumbled on a suspected terrorist lair in a disused shed.

It contained a box stuffed with batteries, wires and balaclava helmets.

Military

There was also a page torn from the phone directory for Taunton in Somerset, revealing Mr Ashdown's address, and a copy of his local newspaper.

This is thought to give dates and venues of his constituency surgeries.

Other documents gave locations of nearly 100 military installations.

Police sealed off the area after scrapyard worker's son Peter Dobson made the discovery at Hayes, Middlesex.

Target

The lair is less than a mile from the bungalow where a man and a woman were arrested on April 13 following the City bomb outrage which killed three people.

It is also within close reach of a lock-up garage where 100lbs of Semtex and six assault rifles were discovered. It had been

Continued on Page 15

WHERE THE PHUKET IS FERGIE?

Fergie .. mystery trip for a "summit" on her marriage

INDIA   PHILIPPINES   THAILAND   PHUKET   NEW GUINEA   BALI   VANUATU   BEDARRA   AUSTRALIA

By ROBERT JOBSON and ANTONELLA LAZZERI

A WORLDWIDE guessing game was under way last night: Where on earth is Fergie?

She has taken her elder daughter out of school and has not been seen in public or at home for a month.

Buckingham Palace refuses to say where she is. But Royal insiders say she jetted off to a paradise resort for a family summit about her troubled marriage to Prince Andrew. Fergie is reported to have stayed in the £510-a-night Amanpuri hotel in Phuket, Thailand, over Easter.

But she is believed to have checked out earlier this week and could now be at any one of a dozen luxury playground resorts.

Possible destinations include Pee Pee in Thailand, Bali in Indonesia, Bedarra Island, Australia, Vanuatu, near Fiji, Verbier, Switzerland, and Necker Island in

Continued on Page 13

Riddle as the Duchess jets off for hol on paradise isle

THE Sun

Friday, June 19, 1992   **25p**   Audited daily sale for May 3,526,87   Today's TV: Pages 36 and 37

Health & F.I.T.N.E.S.S
12-PAGE TREAT FOR YOUR BODY

THE SUN SPEAKS ITS MIND

So sad . . . Gary trudges off

How dare he insult our Gary?

THE sad sight of Gary Lineker trudging off the pitch before the end of England's game with Sweden was a scandal.

He was near to tears at being substituted by manager Graham Taylor. Cruelly disappointed and frustrated. Publicly humiliated.

This was a man who has played his heart out for his country in 80 games.

A man who has been a model for dignified bearing, good humour and modesty in everything he has done.

A hero who courageously captained his country as his tiny son George fought a life-or-death battle
Continued on Page Six

So brave . . . Dad with George

GOTCHA

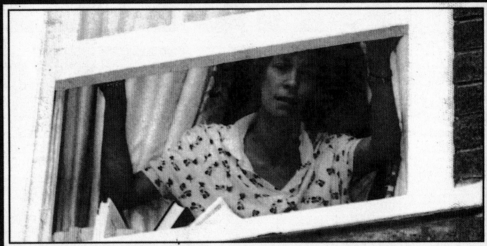

Rude awakening . . . Pandora Maxwell at her window yesterday as police arrive to arrest her husband   **Picture: PAUL WELFORD**

P*** off or I'll call the police | We ARE police Mrs Maxwell

THE wife of Kevin Maxwell yesterday yelled at detectives swooping to arrest her husband: "P*** off, we don't get up for an hour."

Pandora Maxwell, 32, leaned from her bedroom window to tell bemused fraud squad officers: "I'm about to call the police."

A detective retorted: "Madam, we are the police." Pandora, still

By PAUL HOOPER and DAVID WOODING

in her dressing gown, then let the six plain-clothes men into her £1.75million home in Chelsea, London.

The 6.30am raid was the first drama of a day in which Kevin, his brother Ian and a former Maxwell aide were taken to court to face fraud and theft charges totalling £140million. All three

men were on bail last night. Police acted after a six-month investigation into £900million that the Maxwells' tycoon father Robert siphoned from his media empire.

Detectives removed two bags of papers and a lap-top computer in the swoop on 33-year-old Kevin's house. Ian, 36, was arrested at his home in nearby Belgravia which was also searched.

American Larry Trachtenberg, 39, Robert Maxwell's former financial guru, was also held. Kevin

and Ian Maxwell wore smart suits as they were driven to Snow Hill police station, in the City.

It is a stone's throw from the Daily Mirror building — hub of their shattered empire.

Their cheating father held court there before plunging to his death from his yacht last November 5.

After five hours of questioning by officers of the Serious Fraud Office, the Maxwells and

Continued on Page Five

THE Sun

Tuesday, July 21, 1992 **25p** Today's TV: Pages 20 and 21 Audited daily sale for June 3,517,071

PAGE ONE OPINION
When a Minister smeared Paddy

THE Cabinet have got a bee in their bonnet.

They want a Privacy Bill to gag the Press from printing the truth about people in public life.

It's not just the revelations about Virginia Bottomley the unmarried mother, and David Mellor the philanderer, which have upset the Government.

The main plank of their case against the Press is the way Paddy Ashdown was unmasked as an adulterer during the Election campaign.

Well, we've got news for Mr John Major.

Before he accuses the Press of unscrupulous behaviour, he should look closer to home.

In the second week of the General Election campaign, a prominent member of the Cabinet phoned The Sun with the names and addresses of three women.

He claimed they had been having affairs with Mr Ashdown. We were

Continued on Page Six

SHE GAVE A GREAT TOE JOB

Mellor girl's cheeky trick

By DAVID YELLAND

THE actress who had a fling with Minister David Mellor liked sucking men's toes, an ex-lover revealed last night.

City writer Dominic Prince, 31 — a Mellor lookalike — fell for Antonia de Sancha when she was a drama student.

He said: "Sucking guys' toes was all part of her mucking about. I remember spending one night with her on a sofa in her flat.

"She was a delightful eccentric, absolutely beautiful."

Bespectacled Prince, £45,000-a-year acting City editor of the Sunday Express, met half-Spanish Antonia, 30, at a party in 1985.

He said: "My best friend and I were after her, and I guess I got lucky. She was stunning, but after a few hours in her company, you realised she was neurotic.

A pal of Prince said last night:

Continued on Page Four

Stunner Antonia . . . "she was a delightful eccentric"

THE Sun

Wednesday, July 29, 1992   **25p**   Today's TV: Pages 24 and 25   Audited daily sale for June 3,517,071

You'd be wacko to pay for the 27p Mirror's fight with Jacko

THEY don't miss a trick at the ailing Daily Mirror.

First they made their readers stump up another 2p a day to pay for Robert Maxwell's thieving.

Now they're making them foot the Mirror's estimated £5million bill for being sued by Michael Jackson.

That adds up to 250 million of those two pences down the drain.

Why waste 27p a day on the dismal Daily Mirror?

The 25p Sun is a fair price for a great paper.

And it's the one Jacko swears by . . . not at.

LAMONT SACKS JOHN MAJOR

Medal model . . . hunky judo star Ray Stevens in Page 7 Fella pose

Lamont . . . ordered closure

CHANCELLOR Norman Lamont has sacked John Major, The Sun can reveal.

But don't panic folks, the bottom won't fall out of the City — and Mrs Thatcher is not on her way back to Number Ten.

Because this John Major is the Prime Minister's namesake. He is 27, divorced and plays the

EXCLUSIVE
By MIKE CHILVERS

trumpet in his spare time. John will lose his £16,000-a-year post as office manager with Neddy, the National Economic Development Council, when the Government body is wound up on Mr Lamont's orders at the end of the year.

Another 120 colleagues will be

thrown on the dole. Last night John said: "Yes, it's true to say that Norman Lamont has put John Major out of a job."

John's colleagues at the council in Millbank, central London, have managed to see the funny side of the story and joke about the day the Chancellor sacked Mr Major.

A Neddy spokeswoman said: "John took a fair bit of ribbing about his name when he first came here but he's got a good sense of humour and took it all well.

"I remember once when he was trying to book a table at a restaurant they just wouldn't believe him when he said his name was John Major.

"If anyone's looking for an excellent office manager, John Major's your man.

John, from Bromley, Kent, said: "It's doubly ironic because our work at Neddy was finding ways to improve the economy. Now the Government has shut us down and we'll have to find other work."

John, a former Post Office manager, said the

Continued on Page Two

PAGE 7 FELLA GRABS SILVER

SUN Page 7 Fella Ray Stevens won Britain's first Olympic medal in Barcelona last night.

Judo star Ray, 29, scooped a silver as millions of TV viewers cheered at home.

He narrowly missed a gold in the light heavyweight contest. Ray's

By NEIL SYSON

ex-model girlfriend Debbie, 30, yelled: "Come on!" by the arena as he battled Hungarian Antal Covacs.

She said after he lost the 5-minute bout: "I'm disappointed. He

did have it in him to do it — it was so close."

Six-foot Ray wowed Page 7 fans in 1989 and 1990 when he posed in just his judo bottoms. He and Debbie live with son Louis, three, in Kennington, South London.

Full story — Back Page

THE Sun

Friday, August 21, 1992   25p   Today's TV: Pages 32 and 33   Audited daily sale for July 3,503,569

FERGIE'S FINAL BOOB

CINÉ TELE REVUE

By ROBERT JOBSON, Royal Reporter

THIS is the most sensational picture of a Royal ever taken.

It shows topless Fergie flaunting herself in front of Texan beau John Bryan, 37, as they sun themselves in the south of France.

By stripping off in front of the bachelor tycoon, the disgraced Duchess could have made her final boob as a Royal.

The pictures — published in the European TV magazine Cine Tele Revue — reveal the intimate nature of their friendship. And they

Continued on Page Five

MORE AMAZING PICTURES: Pages 4,5,14,15,21,22,23,24

A STRIP TOO FAR...topless Fergie's frolic by the pool with John Bryan is captured in the picture that upset the Queen

25p TO PAY MORE IS IMMORAL...EVEN AT BALMORAL 25p

THE Sun

MELLOR MADE LOVE IN CHELSEA STRIP!

Night he scored four times with actress

By CAROLINE GRAHAM

SULTRY Antonia de Sancha told last night how Cabinet Minister David Mellor made love to her while wearing the Chelsea soccer strip.

Antonia, speaking through a friend, said Mellor appeared from the bathroom of their lovenest in his favourite team's blue and white kit.

The friend said Antonia told her he wore a peaked cap with the Chelsea logo — and the team's socks. Only the shorts were missing.

Antonia, 30, who was waiting naked on the bed, said: "I was too stunned to say anything. "Then he smiled at me, raced across the bedroom and leapt on top of me."

DATE

She said that a week later Minister of Fun Mellor, 43, went to work with the outfit on under his suit before meeting her for another passion session.

Antonia also told pal Joanna Horam Ashbourn how Mellor made love to her four times on the night of their first proper date.

She said she and father-of-two Mellor made love up to five times a week during their three-month affair.

Mellor offered to resign as Minister for National Heritage after the fling became public. Premier John Major refused. Mellor is a close friend of Mr Major, who often joined him to watch Chelsea.

Mellor and his wife Judith were last night due to join Prince Charles and Mr Major at a concert at the Royal Albert Hall.

Four times in a night
— See Pages 4 and 5

Fun .. Mellor as he would look in Chelsea kit

Love .. Antonia yesterday in South of France

After Taylor's Turnips...it's

SPANISH..1 ONIONS..0

What's the point? *England manager Graham Taylor hands out tactics to Nigel Clough in last night's defeat* Picture: **ROGER PARKER**

England down the plug olé

GRAHAM TAYLOR proved last night that he does not know his onions.

This shameful defeat was enough to bring tears to England fans' eyes as Taylor's new-look strikers proved they still do not know the way to goal.

Fonseca's 11th minute goal heaped more pressure on Taylor after this summer's European Championship flop — when the Swedes turned over Taylor's Turnips.

But Taylor last night hit back as TV interviewer Martin Tyler described England's performance as "dismal."

Worse

Taylor snapped: "I disagree with that description and I think it's a very unfair statement to make. I feel it is too strong a condemnation.

"I am not against anyone having an opinion but that is unfair."

Spanish keeper Zubizaretta had just two saves to make — despite Taylor's pre-match pledge to entertain.

And, to make matters

From MARTIN SAMUEL in Santander

worse for the England boss, Norway found the net ten times against tiny San Marino.

That makes a victory in next month's World Cup qualifier at Wembley against the Norwegians doubly vital for Taylor — yet England have won just two of their last nine matches.

Taylor watched in horror

● *Turn to Page 38*

AND AS WE FLOP

WALES	6
FAROES	0
REPUBLIC OF IRELAND	4
LATVIA	0
N.IRELAND	3
ALBANIA	0
NORWAY	10
SAN MARINO	0

37

©News Group Newspapers Ltd. Published and printed by News Group Newspapers Ltd, 1 Virginia St, London E1 9BD; 071-782-4000. Registered as a newspaper at the PO No. 7,103. Austria 21sch, Channel Islands 28p, France 7fr, Germany 2.80dm, Greece 200dr, Italy 1700lt, Portugal 200esc, Spain 200pts, Malta 28c.

9 770307 268045

TAYLOR'S SHAME
SWEDES......2
TURNIPS..1

TAYLOR STUFFED
SPANISH.......1
ONIONS......0

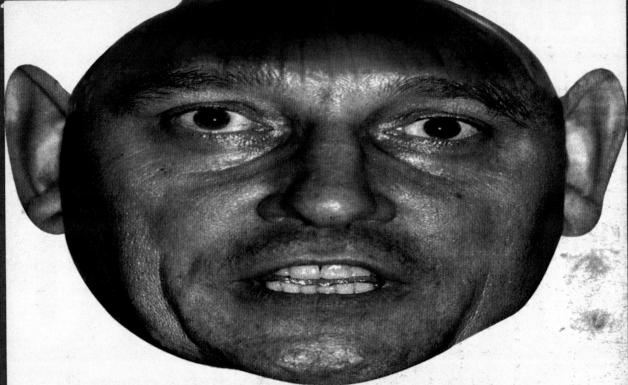

I WONDER WHAT VEGETABLE THEY HAVE IN NORWAY?

GRAHAM TAYLOR has been a turnip. Now he's an onion.

And yesterday the England manager said: "I wonder what bloody vegetable they have in Norway?"

The dilemma hit Taylor — who faces the rampant Norwegians in the World Cup at Wembley next month — as he faced reporters over Wednesday's disaster in Spain.

We dubbed Taylor a turnip when the Swedes bashed his England team 2-1 and put us out of the European Championships.

Now we've turned him into an onion after the Spanish left us weeping.

As Taylor contemplated the time-bomb tie with Norway his mind strayed to the vegetable crisis.

Well, we've got the answer for you, Graham. And a World Cup carrot (that's *gulrot* in Norwegian) is on display in all its glory on Page 46.

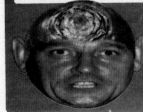

FOR CRYING OUT LOUD GO
SEE PAGE 46

©News Group Newspapers Ltd. Published and printed by News Group Newspapers Ltd. 1 Virginia St, London E1 9BD. 071-782 4000. Registered as a newspaper at the PO No 7,104. Austria 21sch, Channel Islands 26p, France 7fr, Germany 2.60dm, Greece 200dr, Italy 1700lit, Portugal 200esc, Spain 200pts, Malta 26c.

9 770307 268052

37

9am..10% 11.02am..12% 2.18pm..15% 7.43pm..12%

THE GRIN REAPER...Lamont yesterday

Now we've ALL been screwed by the Cabinet

POUND WILL BE DEVALUED: Pages 2 and 3

THE Sun

25p

Don't resign yourself to paying any more

Friday, September 25, 1992　25p　Today's TV: Pages 36 and 37　Audited daily sale for August 3,583,010

MELLOR QUITS AT LAST

TOE JOB TO NO JOB

Out . . . Mellor yesterday after telling the PM: I quit

Actress Antonia . . . three-month fling with Minister

Minister finally sunk by scandals

DAVID MELLOR quit as a Cabinet Minister last night as the scandals over his love life and freebies finally crushed him.

Tory MPs turned on him as his battle for survival threatened to rebound on the Government.

Mellor was forced to admit defeat in the wake of his fling with toe-sucking Antonia de Sancha and foreign trips with blonde Mona Bauwens.

The Minister for Fun said in his

By TREVOR KAVANAGH, Political Editor

resignation letter to John Major: "I do not want to be seen as a liability to you." The Prime Minister told his friend he accepted his decision with "deep regret."

Mellor's wife Judith said last night: "I am very sad that someone with such ability is not able to serve his country in the way he can do best."

Antonia, 31, said: "I'm sorry for him — but he's paying the price for his

indiscretions." Mona, 36, daughter of a top PLO official, said in a statement: "I am very sorry to hear the news."

Details of the Mellors' expenses-paid holiday in Marbella emerged in Mona's High Court libel action last week — and increased the pressure on the Minister to go.

Mona's statement said: "As I explained in court, I invited David and his family to stay as my guests on holiday at a time when I had my own personal problems. I am very grateful

Continued on Page Four

The Sun was FIRST and The Sun was RIGHT

THIS was The Sun's front page on Tuesday when we exclusively revealed Mr Mellor was about to quit. But when quizzed he said: "The Sun made it up like they make up everything."

Say no more.

THE Sun

25P

YOU'LL SAVE TWO PENNIES FOR THE GUY

Friday, October 16, 1992   **25p**   Audited daily sale for September 3,629,893   Today's TV: Pages 28 and 29

PM IN COVER UP ON MINES

He kept job massacre

a secret from Cabinet

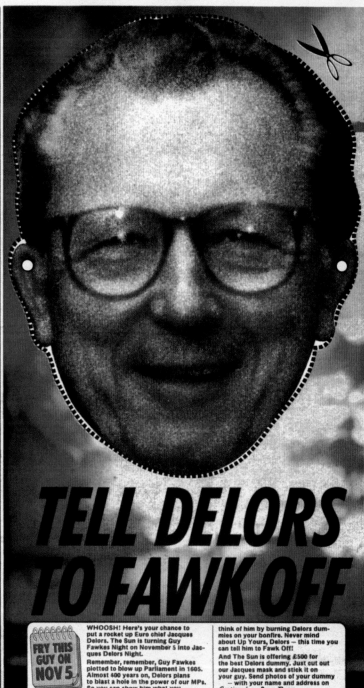

TELL DELORS TO FAWK OFF

By TREVOR KAVANAGH
Political Editor

JOHN Major kept his Cabinet in the dark over the decision to savage the coal industry, it was revealed last night.

The bombshell move to scrap 31 pits and sack 30,000 miners was decided by only a handful of Ministers, including Michael Heseltine and Norman Lamont.

Many of the Cabinet only learned of it from newspaper leaks on the day the cuts were announced.

Premier Mr Major was kept fully informed of the discussions.

He took the final decision to shut the pits last Friday — hours before he unveiled his vision of 1990s Britain to the Tory conference in Brighton.

He has still said nothing in public about the closures.

Last night Tory MPs were furious about what they called Mr Major's "amazing blunder." One

said: "This is an astonishing way to proceed on such a sensitive issue."

Chief Whip Richard Ryder approached backbenchers to gauge reaction to the plan.

Later, the white-faced Tory told a hushed Cabinet: "I think we underestimated the reaction."

Details of the cover-up emerged after the Cabinet was formally told of the programme for the first time at a two-hour meeting yesterday. The plans were formulated by what some MPs call the "underground White-

Continued on Page Two

WHOOSH! Here's your chance to put a rocket up Euro chief Jacques Delors. The Sun is turning Guy Fawkes Night on November 5 into Jacques Delors Night.

Remember, remember, Guy Fawkes plotted to blow up Parliament in 1605. Almost 400 years on, Delors plans to blast a hole in the power of our MPs. So you can show him what you

think of him by burning Delors dummies on your bonfire. Never mind about Up Yours, Delors — this time you can tell him to Fawk Off!

And The Sun is offering £500 for the best Delors dummy. Just cut out our Jacques mask and stick it on your guy. Send photos of your dummy — with your name and address on

Continued on Page Three

FRY THIS GUY ON NOV 5

This page is dedicated to Michael Heseltine. It represents all that he understands about the worries and fears of the ordinary working people in depression-hit Britain. Nothing. Absolutely nothing.

WILL HEZZA SURVIVE PITS SCANDAL? Pages 4 & 5

THE Sun 25p

Wednesday, October 21, 1992   25p   Audited daily sale for September 3,629,893

Lamont . . . five-star comfort

Lamont told to pay up a £900 hotel bill

EXCLUSIVE by PAUL SCOTT

CHANCELLOR Norman Lamont faces another financial crisis — a £900 hotel bill he hasn't paid.

He owes the money for his suite at Brighton's Grand Hotel during the Tory conference.

A staff member said last night: "We think it is hilarious that the man in charge of running the country's finances can't even remember to pay his own bill."

Bosses at the five-star hotel were told and their cashiers have sent Mr Lamont a "pay up" letter.

The embattled Chancellor has been given seven days to settle the account or face legal action.

Speech

His exact bill is £918.30 — comprising £600 for three nights in Suite 827 and the rest for meals, drinks and phone calls.

Mr Lamont spent hours in the fourth-floor suite preparing his conference speech to save his career in the deepening recession.

The hotel worker said: "There were always screwed-up papers all over the floor.

"The maids had to arrange them into little

Continued on Page 12

RUSH FOR SEX AT MIDNIGHT

Mad on her . . . fans queue   **Picture: DAN TOWERS**

Madonna fans in book fever

MADONNA-mania hit the streets last night as 200 fans queued in driving rain to snap up the first copies of her steamy new book Sex.

Some waited for nearly six hours for Sex to go on sale at a shop in London's Covent Garden at a minute past midnight.

Among those rushing to hand over £20 each at Books etc were a honeymoon couple from the US and a fan who said he wanted three copies "in case two wear out."

But while loyal fans braved the weather, the book's official launch turned into a washout.

By DAN COLLINS and PIERS MORGAN

WAIT

Dozens of stars snubbed the £30,000 party at the nearby Mezzunia restaurant.

VIPs including Jonathan Ross, Betty Boo, Vivienne Westwood, Bob Geldof, Richard Branson and Lennie Henry and Dawn French had accepted invitations.

But by midnight only Eurythmics star Dave Stewart, his wife Siobhan Fahey of Shakespear's Sister and Pink Floyd guitarist Dave Gilmour had turned up.

Stewart and Siobhan popped in because he lives nearby — and Gilmour was there because his girlfriend works for the PR firm organising the bash.

Outside in the wet honeymooners Hunter *Continued on Page Three*

Happy honeymooners . . . Hunter and Christina Hyatt waited hours to get Sex   **Picture: DAVE HOGAN**

THE Sun

25p

Wednesday, October 28, 1992   **25p**   Today's TV: Pages 20 and 21   Audited daily sale for September 3,629,893

U TURN-IP

I won't have Sex book in home says Naomi mum

EXCLUSIVE by DAN COLLINS

SUPERMODEL Naomi Campbell's mum has banned Madonna's X-rated book Sex from her house — because of her daughter's kinky poses with the star.

Valerie Campbell, 42, saw the book for the first time yesterday when she was handed a copy by The Sun. After looking at explicit photos of Naomi, 22, romping nude with Madonna, she said: "This is not something I'd have in my house. Similar things appear on TV, but I turn the set off if it comes on.

"It is all right for adults. But I have a seven-year-old son Pierre, Naomi's half-brother.

"If he saw the pictures, I would go round to the house of whoever showed it to him. I would be angry." Sex, which sold

Continued on Page Three

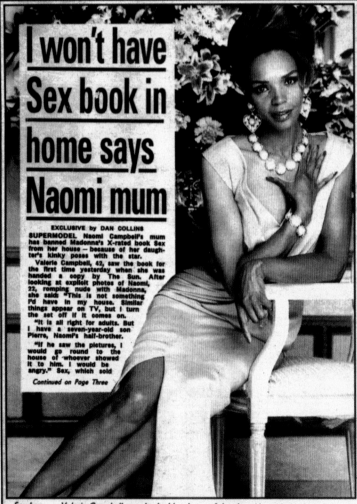

Sex ban . . . Valerie Campbell was shocked by photos of daughter Naomi in Madonna's book

Major drops his poll threat in backdown No4

By TREVOR KAVANAGH and SIMON WALTERS

JOHN MAJOR last night abandoned his threat to call an election if he is defeated by rebel Tory MPs on Europe.

The U-turn came at a tense two-and-a-half hour meeting with the Tory high command in his Downing Street office.

The Prime Minister was warned off by Party chairman Sir Norman Fowler, Lords leader John Wakeham and Chief Whip Richard Ryder.

They told him the Conservative Party would not tolerate a second election just months after winning an outright majority in April.

The PM was also warned he faced defeat at the hands of his own MPs if he insisted on turning Europe into a test of his authority as Premier.

The cave-in is Mr Major's fourth U-turn in six weeks.

He pulled out of the ERM and devalued the pound — after pledging not to. He let shamed Minister David Mellor quit — after vowing to keep him. Then he shelved his decision to

Continued on Page Four

The Sun 25p

Friday, November 6, 1992   **25p**   Today's TV: Pages 32 and 33   Audited daily sale for September 3,629,893

RANDY DICK TRAPPED BY A PIC

Palace admit the rift at last

From ROBERT JOBSON in Seoul

CHARLES and Diana's marriage IS in trouble, a senior Buckingham Palace aide finally confirmed last night.

The Royal aide who masterminded the tour of South Korea made the surprise remark as he complained about media coverage.

Smooth-talking former Foreign Office diplomat Peter Westmacott broke the wall of Palace silence for the first time since speculation began over the marriage.

In an angry outburst to newsmen who quizzed him about the state of the relationship, he admitted: "No, I am not saying the marriage is a happy one, but the treatment has been unfair and exaggerated.

"They have been put under terrible pressure

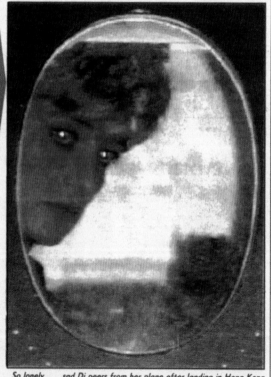

So lonely . . . sad Di peers from her plane after landing in Hong Kong

Continued on Page 11

Lover puts hols snap in wife cheat's local paper

By KIERON SAUNDERS

CHEATING husband Richard Burley was caught out over a holiday affair — when his French lover had their photo printed in his local paper.

Isabelle Pech thought her campsite romeo was single and used the front page to try to track him down after he returned to England suddenly.

But 34-year-old Richard's wife saw the picture — and immediately stormed off. When Isabelle found out the randy trucker was married she went back to France saying: "He is what you call a rat — I never want to see him again."

Lovelorn Isabelle, 25, knew nothing about the man she had a summer fling with, except his first name and that he came from Luton, Beds.

So she appealed to one of the town's papers which published a snap of them with the words "Richard, where are you?"

The young teacher also had thousands of leaflets printed and gave them to passers-by. Devastated Richard said: "I never expected a little holiday to backfire so badly. That's all

Fling . . . snap of Richard and Isabelle

Continued on Page Seven

SEX THREATS TO REBEL TORY MPs—See Page 9

THE SÜN 25P

Monday, November 9, 1992   **25p**   Today's TV: Pages 20 and 21   Audited daily sale for October 3,572,450

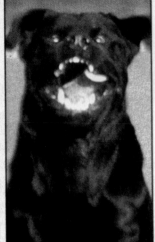

Rottweiler . . . Di's nickname for Camilla

DIANA CALLS

Camilla . . . Prince phoned from yacht

CAMILLA THE ROTTWEILER

EXCLUSIVE: The chapter the world is waiting to read

PRINCESS Diana calls Prince Charles' closest female confidante Camilla Parker Bowles "The Rottweiler," says Royal author Andrew Morton.

The rift between the two women is so deep that Di cannot even bring herself to mention the name of the wife of Brigadier Andrew Parker Bowles.

Morton reveals the depth of the feud in the new paperback version of his best-selling book Diana — Her True Story, published in America this week. Camilla, 45, in turn describes Diana as

By STUART HIGGINS, Deputy Editor

"that ridiculous creature" — a scathing reference to her unpredictable and temperamental behaviour, says Morton.

He writes in the book: "There is no love lost between these two women locked into an eternal triangle of rivalry.

"Diana calls her rival 'The Rottweiler' while Camilla refers to the Princess as 'that ridiculous creature.'" Diana, 31, refuses to acknowledge the woman she blames for the breakdown of her marriage. Three weeks ago she snubbed Camilla

at a service for El Alamein veterans. Diana's suspicions about her husband's friendship with Camilla were inflamed when she accidentally "eavesdropped" on Charles as he made a secret ship-to-shore call to his old flame.

It happened during this summer's family holiday aboard Greek billionaire John Latsis's yacht the Alexander. The Mediterranean trip had been described as a "second honeymoon."

Morton tells how Diana "stumbled" across her husband making his furtive call via satellite link to the Wiltshire country home of the woman who was once considered to be a potential wife. The

Continued on Page Two

Book . . . revelations

THE Sun 25p

Wednesday, November 25, 1992   **25p**   Today's TV: Pages 20 and 21   Audited daily sale for October 3,572,450

ONE'S BUM YEAR

Mandy's fib costs her £5m

EXCLUSIVE by ANDY COULSON

MANDY Smith abandoned her £5million court battle with ex-husband Bill Wyman yesterday after being caught telling fibs in the witness box.

The former model had to settle for just £580,000 from the multi-millionaire Rolling Stone when it was revealed Hello! magazine had secretly paid her a "substantial" fee for a series of articles.

During three days of questioning about her earnings, Mandy, 22, had denied a deal.

But Wyman's team of lawyers produced documents proving cash had changed hands — and leaving Mandy's case in tatters.

Her legal advisers realised any hope of getting a major slice of the star's estimated £24million fortune had been destroyed.

Last night Mandy — who first dated 56-year-old Wyman when she was just 13 — was said to be "hugely disappointed."

But she could have been charged with perjury.

After the revelations, the seven-day High Court hearing was halted. A deal was struck which left Mandy

Continued on Page Nine

Court out . . . blonde Mandy yesterday

Or as Queen admits: I've had an *Annus Horribilis*

I know how you feel Ma'am   Troubled John Major leans over the Lord Mayor to speak to the Queen

THE Queen opened her heart to the nation yesterday — and admitted 1992 has been one of her worst years ever.

In the most revealing speech of her 40-year reign, she said: "It has turned out to be an annus horribilis" — Latin for a horrible year.

Her remarks came after a year in which she has seen

By RUKI SAYID

Charles' and Andrew's marriages hit the rocks, Anne's end in divorce and the blaze at her beloved Windsor Castle.

The Queen also signalled she is ready to start paying income tax on her estimated £6billion fortune.

Following the barrage of public criticism, she said: "This sort of questioning can act — and it should do so — as an effective engine for change."

Looking weary and fighting a heavy cold, the Queen made her astonishing speech at a banquet in London's Guildhall to mark her 40th year on the throne.

Guests including Premier John Major heard her say: "1992 is not a year on which I shall look back with undiluted pleasure. In the words of one of my more sympathetic correspondents it has turned out to be an annus horribilis." In a

Continued on Page Four

THE Sun

XXVp

25p NEWSPAPER OF THE ANNUS

Thursday, November 26, 1992 **25p** Today's TV: Pages 36 and 37 Audited daily sale for October 3,572,450

LAMONT AND HIS UNPAID CREDIT CARD

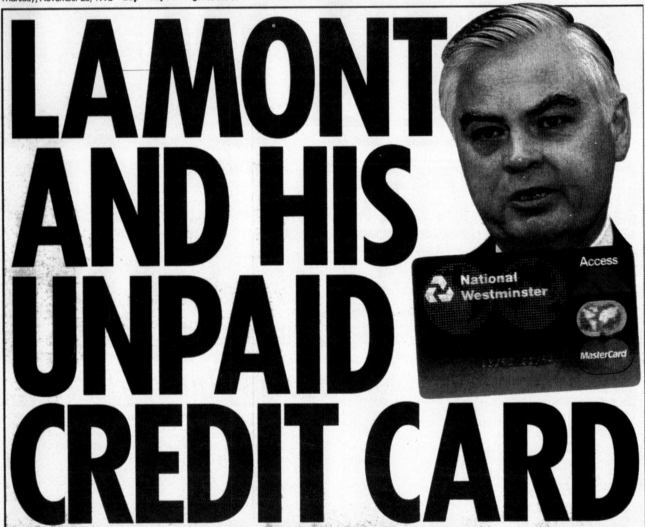

● Over his limit 22 times

● Five legal warning letters

SUN EXCLUSIVE by SIMON WORTHINGTON

CHANCELLOR Norman Lamont has been sent five legal warning letters by Access for not making monthly payments, The Sun can reveal today.

He is currently £470 over his £2,000 spending limit — and shopkeepers will be told not to accept his credit card again until he has paid some of it off.

Mr Lamont, 50, who earns £63,047 a year, has gone over his credit limit 22 times since he got his Access card through the National Westminster Bank nearly eight years ago.

The deadline for paying his October statement expired on Sunday without a cheque being received at Access's Southend HQ. A sixth warning is expected to be sent to him at 11 Downing Street within days.

The first went to Mr Lamont as he was putting the finishing touches to last year's Budget.

Cabinet colleagues will be extremely embarrassed by the revelation and the Chancellor is bound to face questions over his financial competence, since it is his job to administer the nation's finances.

Last night a banking analyst said: "No wonder Britain is in a recession if Mr Lamont runs the country like he runs his own bank account.

"He has presided over the collapse of the economy while his personal finances are in disarray. His reputation as guardian of the country's economic future must now be severely questioned."

A National Westminster insider told The Sun: "He has been in and out of arrears since he got the card. Another letter is about to go out to him warning he has 14 days to pay."

Mr Lamont used the card as recently as Monday of last week, when he spent £17.47 at a Thresher off-licence near Paddington, West London. The small amount meant the assistant did not need to phone Access for authorisation.

If he had called, staff would have told him to refuse to accept the card.

SUMMONS

Usually Access legal department is involved if an account stays over limit for more than 60 days. Two letters would be sent demanding payment within 14 days.

If the customer fails to pay, a county court summons or an outside debt collection agency is then used.

Mr Lamont's VIP status means that his account is handled by a senior manager. Any normal customer would face a less tolerant attitude.

It is normal banking practice to alert customers who go over the agreed limit. They are told: "Your account is seriously in

Continued on Page Two

THE Sun

25p TAX FREE

NEWSPAPER OF THE ANNUS

Friday, November 27, 1992   **25p**   Today's TV: Pages 32 and 33   Audited daily sale for October 3,572,450

YOU SPOKE

PAGE ONE OPINION

The Queen pays tax and it's a victory for people power...

THE people spoke and the Monarch listened.

For the first time, the Queen has bowed to the wishes of her subjects.

It is a gracious acknowledgement of public disquiet which The Sun applauds.

A Sun phone poll two months ago showed 90 per cent of you wanted the Monarch to pay income tax on her personal fortune.

By agreeing, the Queen takes a momentous step towards the 21st century.

Lucky

Soon we will see a new-look Royal Family, with the army of hangers-on supported by the Monarch, not the taxpayer.

It is a reform that is welcome, even if it has been one heck of a time coming.

For too long we have looked back to the glorious, golden times of yesteryear.

To the days of the Empire, when privilege was an unquestioned

Continued on Page Six

Pay as you reign . . . the Queen's decision to pay income tax could cost her £12million a year

SHE LISTENED

THE Sun

25p

Thursday, December 10, 1992   **25p** Today's TV: Pages **40** and **41**   Estimated daily sale for November 3,514,867

THRONE ALONE

MPs say Charles won't be King, Di won't be Queen. It's down to Wills

CHARLES and Diana's plans to become King and Queen despite their official separation are doomed, MPs said last night.

Westminster was united in predicting the Prince will have to step aside and leave eldest son William to take the throne alone.

MPs of all parties said it was inconceivable the estranged pair could be crowned and carry out Royal duties as a couple.

By TREVOR KAVANAGH and SIMON WALTERS

They gasped in disbelief as John Major claimed, after officially announcing the separation, that it would not stop Di becoming Queen.

He told the Commons: "The succession to the throne is unaffected. There is no reason why the Princess of Wales should not be Queen in due course."

The Premier was backed by Buckingham Palace, which said

the couple would not divorce. A spokesman said Charles' commitment to his duties as heir was "undiminished" and stressed: "There is no question of either party standing down."

But Tory MP Tony Marlow said: *"We cannot allow Diana to become Queen, even if it means taking the throne off Charles. It would destroy the Monarchy."*

Fellow Tory Elizabeth Peacock said: "The most obvious Continued on Page Seven

It's over . . . but Diana and Charles both looked cheerful yesterday as the country was told of the official separation

28-PAGE SPECIAL WITH ANDREW MORTON'S PICTURE DIARY

THE Sun 25p

Saturday, December 12, 1992   25p   Audited daily sale for November 3,515,236

Visit . . . Mrs Bottomley

Virginia Bottomley's mum waits 7 hours in agony for hospital op

Exclusive

By JOHN KAY

THE mother of Health Secretary **Virginia Bottomley** was kept waiting in agony for seven hours for an op at an NHS hospital.

Mrs Barbara Garnett, 74, was forced to sit in the casualty department because of a bed shortage.

But Mrs Garnett, who later had an operation, never tried to queue-jump by saying who her daughter was.

The family link was discovered by staff only after Mrs Garnett was admitted.

Mrs Bottomley, 44, who is planning to close or merge up to 15 London hospitals, visited her mother on Thursday night hours after the operation.

She was "most impressed" with her mother's treatment.

Mrs Garnett was taken to the Queen Mary's hospital, Roehampton, South-West London on Wednesday after complaining of severe stomach pains.

A Department of Health spokesman said: "Mrs Garnett's family doctor drove her to the hospital because she was feeling unwell.

"She was taken to the accident and emergency depart-

Continued on Page Eight

I WILL BE KING I WON'T REMARRY

Charles rules . . . determined to be King

Charles promises to make duty his life

EXCLUSIVE

By TREVOR KAVANAGH
POLITICAL EDITOR

PRINCE Charles has stepped in to stop the constitutional crisis over his split from Diana by declaring: "I WILL be the next King."

He also promised he will "never re-marry" because of his determination to fulfil his Royal destiny.

His remarkable vows were made in a series of phone calls to a circle of friends and acquaintances close to 10 Downing Street.

The friends say Charles will now devote his life to duty with the sole aim of eventually taking over from the Queen and serving his country.

The Sun understands the Prince asked top lawyer Lord Goodman about the constitutional position on his rights to the Throne.

He was advised that divorce would be no barrier to him succeeding to the Throne — but a second marriage would not be acceptable.

Charles has also strenuously ruled out any suggestion that he should renounce his right to the Throne in favour of his elder son William.

A close friend of Charles said last night: "Already it is possible to see the change in the Prince of Wales' demeanour simply by looking at his face.

"His unhappy marriage and his constant battles with the Princess have clouded his vision of the future for so long that he has been indecisive about his role and duty within the monarchy. In the last few weeks, since he has known his marriage was over, his mind has cleared.

"He no longer has the daily encumbrance of thinking about his wife all the time. He can concentrate on his job.

"The Prince has reacted quickly because he wants to quell the constitutional crisis over the

Continued on Page Five

VIRGIN SCREWS BA

Virgin

Branson wins £610,000 libel damages, £1m legal costs and a public apology

Richard Branson . . . victory over BA "dirty tricks" war

EXCLUSIVE by DAVID YELLAND
City Editor

VIRGIN Airlines boss Richard Branson has won a sensational £3.5million "dirty tricks" war with arch rivals British Airways.

Mighty BA are to pay him £610,000 libel damages, foot Virgin's £1million legal bill — and make an "abject" public apology to Branson.

BA must also meet its own legal costs of about £2million.

It is a stunning victory for the little guy who refused to knuckle under to what he saw as a "dirty tricks" campaign by British Airways to destroy his eight-plane airline.

One senior BA source admitted last night: "It is a total humiliation for us — and a total victory for Branson."

The climbdown allows BA to avoid a vicious libel court action due to start on Monday and scheduled to last 12 weeks.

Branson took them to court,

claiming they accused him of lying over his allegations of a dirty tricks campaign.

He had said BA poached passengers, sometimes as they queued to buy Virgin tickets at New York's JFK airport.

TOUGH

Branson also alleged BA shredded documents he subpoenaed for a U.S. court action under anti-trust laws. And he said the giant airline ran a "dirty tricks" Press campaign against him.

It would have been one of the most dramatic libel trials in history with Branson's QC George Carman ripping into BA chairman Lord King in the witness box.

Branson's case concerned an article in BA News, an in-house magazine, in March last year. In it, King

accused Branson of making up his allegations to get publicity.

Now BA will simply throw in the towel. Its apology has been sent to the judge presiding over the case, Mr Justice Drake. He has to agree the wording.

It is BA's worst defeat since 1985 when it admitted trying to put Sir Freddie Laker's Skytrain airline out of business. That debacle cost BA £5.75million.

Branson had claimed that a prime mover behind the BA campaign was its millionaire PR adviser Brian Basham.

Basham insists he fought tough but fair and is threatening to sue BA if they now dump on him in their apology to Branson.

He said: "I am mystified by this climbdown by British Airways. The Press campaign I was involved with was fair and decent.

"I am loyal to British Airways but I must protect my reputation. I will

Continued on Page Seven

THE Sun 25p

Thursday, January 14, 1993   25p   Today's TV: Pages 32 and 33

THE BIG DEBATE OVER CAMILLAGATE
Today you decide if The Sun publishes the tapes—Page 7

SPANK YOU

& GOODNIGHT

Bombers humble Saddam in 30 minutes

MORE than 100 Allied jets yesterday gave tyrant Saddam Hussein a spanking — blasting missile sites in a raid that took just 30 minutes.

Four RAF Tornados based in Saudi Arabia joined the attack.

They helped U.S. warplanes from the carrier Kitty Hawk and French jets to blitz rocket and radar centres in Southern

By NICK PARKER

Iraq. The raid followed weeks of "cheat and retreat" provocations by Saddam to test out the resolve of the United Nations. After the blitz he immediately caved in to two UN demands — to stop raids on Kuwait and allow UN flights into Iraq.

One aide of U.S. President Bush said:

"It's just a spanking for Saddam, not a real beating."

British sources said Saddam was given a "short, sharp and telling lesson."

The Allied strike force — led by Stealth bombers — was airborne for 2¾ hours to set up the 30-minute raid. All planes returned safely despite Iraqi rocket and anti-aircraft fire.

The raid was almost exactly two years after the start of the Gulf War — and

followed a day of tension in which U.S. Secretary of State Lawrence Eagleburger said Saddam's recent behaviour was "insane." He had been sending jets and missiles into the UN's no-fly zone in Southern Iraq.

President Bush's aide Marlin Fitzwater said America had not considered targeting Saddam personally yesterday — because the UN had not authorised such action.

Full amazing story — Pages Two and Three

THE Sun 25p

Friday, January 29, 1993   25p   Today's TV: Pages 36 and 37   Estimated daily sale last week 3,543,413

WRIT HITS THE FAN

Defiant Major stakes his career on libel case

Party time . . . caterer Clare Latimer pours John Major a drink at a Downing Street reception

DEFIANT John Major put his Premiership on the line yesterday by slapping libel writs on two magazines.

Similar writs were issued by unmarried Clare Latimer, 41, whose name has been linked with the Prime Minister's in false rumours.

Mr Major is furious over suggestions of an "association" with Miss Latimer, owner of Downing Street caterers Clare's Kitchen.

By TREVOR KAVANAGH, Political Editor and JOHN KAY

He is ready to go into the witness box to deny that he has had an affair with her. It would make him the first British Prime Minister in history to give evidence in a libel hearing.

Senior ministers believe the magazines — the Left-wing New Statesman and the satirical rag Scallywag — are bluffing by insisting they will fight the case through the High Court. But they know that libel juries can produce surprise verdicts. Anything less than a unanimous judgment with acceptable damages against the magazines could rebound on Mr Major.

One close friend said last night: "It will be the trial of the century if the Prime Minister goes into the witness box. The last thing we would want is a split decision or nominal damages."

Ministers are counting on a complete apology from the editors and publishers, coupled with substantial out-of-court damages which Mr Major, 49, would give to charity. They are confident that, if the case does go to court, Mr Major will score a resounding victory.

Lawyers last night predicted he could win damages of up to £500,000 if his libel actions are successful.

Mr Major has agreed to meet the costs of bringing the actions himself. The bill could be up to £100,000.

His solicitors, Biddle and Company, will hire top barristers and libel experts if the case goes to court. If Mr Major loses, the

Continued on Page Two

The Sun

25P

Friday, February 19, 1993   25p   Today's TV: Pages 32 and 33   Audited daily sale for January 3,557,751

3m dole queue stretches to Sicily

By TREVOR KAVANAGH,
Political Editor,
and MARK SOLOMONS

BRITAIN'S dole queue topped three million yesterday — enough people to stretch from London to Sicily.

Unemployment figures soared past the grim milestone for the first time in almost six years.

Another 78,726 workers lost their jobs last month — taking the total to 3,062,065.

If all those unemployed stood in line they would form a queue 1,160 miles long.

That's from London to a point 33 miles beyond the Sicilian capital Palermo — or London to within two miles of Reykjavik, Iceland.

The unadjusted figure for total jobless was the highest since April 1987. January was the 33rd month in a row that unemployment had risen.

The dismal statistics sparked fury across the country and uproar in the Commons.

As thousands of demonstrators converged on Westminster, Labour leader John Smith accused John Major of "standing

Continued on Page Four

JAMIE: NEW PICTURE OF HIS KILLERS
See Centre Pages

MAN WHO MADE LOVE TO PAVEMENTS

Watkins . . . he took down his pants to make love to pavements

He even had a go at an underpass

— COURT TOLD

A YOUNG electrician could not curb his kinky passion for pavements, a court heard yesterday.

Karl Watkins, 20, repeatedly lay face-down on them with his underpants and trousers round his ankles.

He was caught having sex with pavements, footpaths and even an underpass.

Watkins continued his bizarre behaviour despite

By JOHN SCOTT

being arrested twice. He was spotted falling for flagstones near his home in Redditch, Worcestershire, six times in ten months.

Women and young children saw him at it, Hereford Crown Court heard.

Prosecutor Ian Morris said: "He had a girlfriend and gave the impression of being a wholly unexceptional man.

"But there is a strange and dark side to his character which made him commit indecent and bizarre acts in public.

"These were motivated by a desire for sexual gratification."

LEWD

Watkins was convicted of five charges of outraging public decency by committing acts of a lewd, disgusting and obscene nature.

He had denied all offences

during a three-day trial in which several witnesses, including children, gave evidence from behind a screen.

One 11-year-old boy described seeing Watkins' bare bottom "moving up and down as if he was humping the pavement."

A mother said: "I was totally shocked. There were young children about at the time."

Watkins claimed the witnesses were either mistaken

Continued on Page Two

TO PAVEMENTS

THE Sun 25p

Thursday, February 25, 1993 **25p** Today's TV: Pages 28 and 29 Audited daily sale for January 3,557,751

Bobby Moore

A TRUE HERO WHO'LL NEVER BE FORGOTTEN

By JOHN KAY

BOBBY Moore was a shy man with a voice like a gentle whisper.

But he was a golden-haired giant among men and touched all our lives.

Bobby came from a council house in the tough back streets of East London to leave his mark on history.

His sense of decency and honour as a footballer went beyond the pitch and made him a real-life Boys' Own hero.

Bobby's death early yesterday at the age of 51 from liver cancer leaves Britain and the world a good deal poorer. Fans at League games last night showed their respect by standing for a minute's silence.

Hundreds of supporters of Bobby's West Ham club piled scarves and flowers at the gates of the Upton Park ground.

His triumph when he led England to its 4-2 victory over West Germany in the 1966 World Cup will never be forgotten.

Bobby Charlton, Moore's team-mate in that winning team, explained Bobby's lasting appeal in his tribute:

"He was a gentleman. He was very kind, very courteous, very thoughtful and did things with great dignity. He was a truly lovely man."

Pele, Bobby's greatest opponent on the football field but a great friend off it, almost broke down in tears when told of his death by The Sun last night.

He said: "I am so, so sorry — as I know the whole world will be. He was such a wonderful, wonderful man."

As Prime Minister John Major said from the heart last night: "Bobby was one of the immortals. He will be

Continued on Page Two

Sun TRIBUTE TO THE GREATEST

THE Sun is to organise a glittering testimonial soccer match in honour of Bobby Moore.

The game — which we plan for Wembley — will be a tribute to the World Cup captain and raise money for his family and charity.

It will be between an England All-Star XI and a Rest Of The World side. Last night one of Bobby's 1966 team-mates, former striker Bobby Charlton, said: "It's a fantastic idea."

We want all the Cup-winning England side and ex-manager Sir Alf Ramsey to turn out for

Continued on Page Four

SPECIAL EDITION: PAGES 2,3,4,5,9,37,38,39,40 PLUS 4-PAGE PULLOUT

THE Sun

25p

EVERY BIT HELPS ON A TIGHT BUDGET

Wednesday, March 17, 1993   25p   Today's TV: Pages 24 and 25   Audited daily sale for February 3,536,069

NIGHTMARE ON NORM STREET

FRIGHTENER...Lamont's Budget has more horrors than Freddie Kruger

- ## £17 billion tax hike
- ## Gas, electric shock
- ## Home loans blow

By TREVOR KAVANAGH, Political Editor

CHANCELLOR Norman Lamont last night hit every home in Britain by dropping a sensational £17billion tax timebomb.

His nightmare Budget hammers householders, motorists, smokers and everyone with a job.

It means a couple making £16,500 a year will be £8.50 a week worse off next year. A couple on £30,000 will be over £15 a week worse off.

The Chancellor delivered his biggest shock by slapping VAT on gas, electricity, coal and heating oil used in the home. Tory MPs gasped as he also slashed mortgage tax relief and ordered immediate price rises on petrol, booze and cigarettes.

Mr Lamont, desperate to stop state spending soaring out of control, will phase in his "Spend Now, Pay Later" Budget moves between now and 1995.

The bill for taxpayers will be huge — £6.5billion next year and £10.5billion the year after. That is equal to an 11p jump in income tax over two years.

But it helps Mr Lamont to boost small businesses and hand out a £230million package of incentives to employers to

Continued on Page Two

WORLD EXCLUSIVE

I'VE MESSED UP MY LIFE

Fergie . . surrounded by photos of Andrew   **Picture: ARTHUR EDWARDS**

For the first time since the separation, Fergie opens her heart about growing up, mistakes and saying sorry

By JUDY WADE

THE Duchess of York has bravely admitted for the first time: "I've messed up my life."

In an astonishingly frank interview with The Sun, Fergie said she wanted to say: "I'm sorry."

And she poured out her heart about her life, her past and her hopes for the future.

She talked at her home in Wentworth, Surrey, surrounded by pictures of her estranged husband, Prince Andrew.

The antique desk she works at is almost a shrine to the Duke of York. The largest photograph facing her is a huge portrait of the sailor prince. And standing out from all the others as a monument to a lost love is their wedding photograph.

Fergie explained candidly: "Life is about growing up. We all have to grow up.

"We all make serious mistakes and we learn by them. And that's

Continued on Centre Pages

THE *Fergie* INTERVIEW: Pages 23, 24 & 25

Di ... she beamed

Charles and Di exchange cheeky kisses

By ROBERT JOBSON
Royal Reporter

CHARLES and Diana kissed each other last night for the first time since they split up.

HE gave her a smacker on each cheek as they bumped into each other at a banquet.

And SHE repaid the compliment with an identical salute.

The last time they kissed in public was at Lady Helen Windsor's wedding last year.

Last night's show of affection happened after the Royal couple arrived separately for the bash at the Portuguese embassy in London.

Diana chatted to one group of guests, while Charles stood talking to another.

As the 31-year-old Princess prepared to enter the embassy's Grand Hall, Charles smiled at his estranged wife.

Then he stepped forward and kissed her.

Di beamed back and did the same to him.

The banquet was thrown by Portugal's President Mario Soares, who is on a state visit.

Earlier, Di kept Charles waiting when she arrived late.

He had to sit in his car for five minutes until she turned up.

Protocol decrees that Diana must arrive before her husband because

Continued on Page Two

After 231 years Buck House is open to the public

NOT IN HERE I'M ON THE THRONE

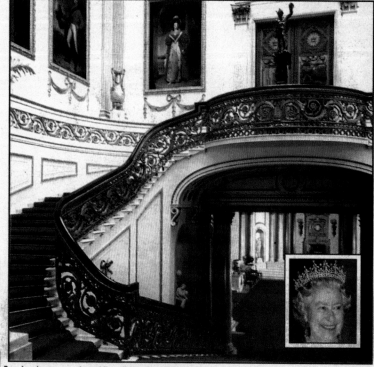

Royal welcome ... the public will be allowed on the Palace's Entree Staircase, thanks to the Queen

By TREVOR KAVANAGH, Political Editor

THE Queen is throwing open Buckingham Palace to the public for the first time.

Millions will pay £8 a head to visit the greatest tourist show on earth.

They will see fabulous royal riches — including the Throne Room.

But anyone hoping to glimpse the Queen will be disappointed. Her private apartments will be out of bounds.

And the Palace will be open only during August and September, time of the traditional royal break at Balmoral.

It was the Queen's idea to let in the public. She hopes to raise £30-£40million in five years to repair fire damage at Windsor Castle.

The Palace, the Royals' London home for 231 years, is expected to attract 400,000 visitors this year alone, it

Continued on Page Two

THE Sun

25p

EastEnders 3 TIMES A WEEK
See Page 21

Star. . .Letitia Dean

Thursday, May 6, 1993   25p   Today's TV: Pages 32 and 33   Estimated daily sale for March 4,032,817(including Today)

> ❝ **Five times a night? Once is enough if you do it right** ❞
> *Says ASIL NADIR*

ASIL ASIT OFF

Amazing sex life of fugitive tycoon. He would keep 8 girls happy

Runaway Asil Nadir . . . girl said he loved rough sex

Lover Abide Gonultas . . . flew out to Cyprus with Polly Peck boss

EXCLUSIVE By KIERON SAUNDERS

FUGITIVE tycoon Asil Nadir was so randy he had eight girlfriends on the go at the same time, one of his minders said last night.

Each of his "harem" had a different personality and Nadir would choose which one to romp with according to his mood.

Bodyguard Sandy Grant told how Turkish-Cypriot Nadir's insatiable desire for sex increased as his Polly Peck empire slid towards debts of more than £1billion.

Last night Nadir, 52, was celebrating in Northern Cyprus after flitting from Britain to escape false accounting charges totalling £30million.

He jumped his £3.5million bail and is thought to have flown out, disguised in a wig, on a hired plane from Hatfield airfield, Herts. With him was one of his eight women, secretary Abide Gonultas, 24.

Minder Sandy was one of three armed ex-Royal Marines whose duties included shuffling women in and out of Nadir's £3million townhouse in Mayfair, London, without them spotting each other.

Shaven-haired Sandy, 36, said: "When it came to sex he was like a lot of blokes. It was wham and bam. One of his girls told me he was bloody rough in bed."

Sandy, 6ft 3ins and 19st, added: "The only comment I ever heard him make about his love life was when I was going on at the chauffeur one day about Burton boss Ralph Halpern and his five-times-a-night bonking sessions. Asil just said, 'If you do it right, once is enough.' "

Sandy, who earned £3,000-a-month during two years as Nadir's round-the-clock minder, told how the divorced tycoon's lust increased as his company headed for for the rocks. He said:

❝ He had a tremendous sex drive. I suppose it was as fierce as the drive that put him at the top in business.

But it seemed to go into overdrive when the troubles began. Sometimes it was like a farce at his home or office, keeping the

Continued on Page Two

THE Sun

25p

Thursday, June 10, 1993   **25p**   Today's TV: Pages 36 and 37   Audited daily sale for April 4,081,624 (including Today)

ONE FOOT IN

THE GREYVE

THE STARS AND TRIPE

U.S.A. 2 ENGLAND 0

ENGLAND dropped a star-spangled clanger last night as Graham Taylor's cowboys were scalped by the braves of the USA.

Taylor's team was expected to cruise to victory over the part-time Yanks in the USA Cup match at Foxboro, near Boston. But they flopped in one of the biggest upsets since America beat England in the 1950 World Cup in Brazil.

Full story . . . Back Page

Shamed . . . England boss Taylor

Major is finished as Lamont plunges knife

By TREVOR KAVANAGH, Political Editor

JOHN Major is finished as Prime Minister after sacked Chancellor Norman Lamont's sensational Commons revenge attack, Tory MPs said last night.

His hopes of hanging on to office were destroyed as Mr Lamont delivered a calculated political assassination on his former boss and pal.

Mr Lamont's wife Rosemary, who was sitting in the public gallery, urged her husband to retaliate and helped write the devastating speech.

Backbenchers gasped as Mr Major's grey personality and politics were torn to shreds by the man who helped put him in Downing Street.

Mr Lamont branded Mr Major a ditherer who changed his mind every day and was more interested in cheap headlines than principles.

He went on: "We give the impression of being in office but not in power.

"Far too many decisions are made for 36 hours' publicity."

Mr Lamont declared: "I believe in politics you should decide what is right and then decide the presentation, and not the other way round.

"Unless this approach is changed, this Government will not survive and does not deserve to survive." Mr Lamont accused the Prime

Continued on Page Two

Nine pages of SunSport

YANKS 2 PLANKS 0

Taylor MUST go

From BRIAN WOOLNOUGH
U.S.A. 2 England 0

GRAHAM TAYLOR'S public humiliation and shame was completed here last night.

His England side were outplayed, outclassed and well and truly beaten by a team of soccer second-raters.

Now Taylor surely HAS to go.

When the killer second goal went in midway through the second half Taylor's career was all but over.

And his expression told the whole story — he looks a broken man.

Millions of armchair viewers could not believe it as the Americans cut through England with ease.

It could have been 4-0 at half-time, such was the poor defending of England, the missed passing and the total lack of penetration up front.

Taylor's World Cup nightmare had followed him all the way to Foxboro.

Not even the boost of knowing that World Cup rivals Holland had dropped a vital point at home to Norway could lift England in front of an interested and then excited U.S.A. crowd.

It could have been 2-0 in the opening eight minutes, there were other chances for the Americans and what has happened to England in the last seven days does not bear thinking about.

From a side still hopeful of qualifying for the World Cup we have disappeared under Taylor into a rabble that you feel embarrassed to watch representing the country.

Despair

America had beaten only Saudi Arabia in 16 matches this season and their 44th-minute goal was their first for 346 minutes.

The architect was Roy Wegerle, the Coventry striker who teased and toyed with England's defence throughout the game.

Wegerle's run caused confusion, Jeff Agoos crossed deep to the far post, Tab Ramos hooked it back and there was Thomas Dooley bending to head in.

The goal was overdue as the gloom and despair continued.

Last night England were not headless chickens, they were hopeless footballers.

And worse was to come when Chris Woods missed a corner and sub-

● Turn to Page 46

QUIT NOW . . . Graham Taylor's career is surely all but over

England handed new Cup lifeline

From PAT SHEEHAN
Holland 0 Norway 0

GRAHAM TAYLOR, the England manager who landed in a pile of Norse manure, came up smelling of roses in Rotterdam.

Taylor created a stink with two World Cup disasters in Poland and Norway.

But last night the Norsemen, who inflicted a humiliating 2-0 defeat on England in Oslo, came to his rescue.

If Holland had won, Taylor could have virtually kissed goodbye to the finals in America next year.

But if his side can now grab five points out of six in their last three games, and keep a grip on their one-goal advantage in goal difference over Holland, they can make it after all.

Taylor, in Boston on England's U.S. tour, said: "As far as I'm concerned the

GROUP 2 TABLE

	P	W	D	L	F	A	Pts
Norway	7	5	2	0	20	3	12
England	7	3	3	1	16	6	9
Holland	7	3	3	1	17	8	9
Poland	5	3	2	0	8	3	8
Turkey	8	1	1	6	7	17	3
S Marino	8	0	1	7	1	32	1

TO PLAY: Sept 8.- England v Poland. Sept 22.- San Marino v Holland, Norway v Poland. Oct 13.- Holland v England, Poland v Turkey. Oct 27.- Turkey v Poland. Nov 10.- Turkey v Norway. Nov 16.- San Marino v England. Nov 17.- Poland v Holland.

position remains the same. It's in our hands. If we win all three matches we will qualify."

His No2 Lawrie McMenemy, with the Under-21 side in France, added: "It is a result that will lift the England camp. It's good news and any good news is welcome at the moment!

"We are still confident of making it to the finals and this has certainly helped."

Disappointed Dutch manager Dick Advocaat said: "Norway are on their way. Now it is a battle between us and England for the second position."

The Dutch missed a string of chances last night and even Norway boss Egil Olsen admitted: "We were lucky."

It's easy for Einstein. Is it for you?

	2		1	3
3		3		1
3	4	3		2
		2	2	
2	3	2	5	2

Each line of 5 numbers must total 14. Place a number into each empty square to solve the puzzle.

If you can manage it without a calculator you could be eligible to join Mensa, The High IQ Society. Simply fill in the coupon below for further details and a copy of the self administered test.

©News Group Newspapers Ltd. Published and printed by News Group Newspapers Ltd, 1 Virginia St, London E1 9BD, 071-782-4000. Registered as a newspaper at the PO No. 7,332. Austria 21sch, Channel Islands 26p, France 7fr, Germany 2.80dm, Greece 250dr, Italy 2000L, Portugal 200esc, Spain 200pts, Malta 20c.

9 900372 200750

HAGAR THE HORRIBLE

By CHRIS BROWNE

WOULD YOU LIKE SOME STRAINED SPINACH, LITTLE DRAGON BABY?

I'LL TAKE THAT AS A "NO"